New Women Poets

EDITED BY
CAROL RUMENS

BLOODAXE BOOKS

ISBN: 1 85224 145 4

First published 1990 by
Bloodaxe Books Ltd,
P.O. Box 1SN,
Newcastle upon Tyne NE99 1SN.

Second impression 1993.

Bloodaxe Books Ltd acknowledges
the financial assistance of Northern Arts.

Typesetting by Bryan Williamson, Darwen, Lancashire.

Cover printing by J. Thomson Colour Printers Ltd, Glasgow.

Printed in Great Britain by
Cromwell Press Ltd, Broughton Gifford, Melksham, Wiltshire.

Contents

10   *Introduction* by CAROL RUMENS

Eva Salzman
17   The English Earthquake
18   Ending up in Kent
19   With Steve Ovett in Preston Park
19   Rain in New York
21   Cheap Thrills
22   Horoscope
22   Birds Courting Loudly
23   Soliloquy
24   Time Out
25   Power Games

Linda France
26   If Love Was Jazz
27   Hennaing My Hair
28   Elementary
29   Gate-crasher
30   Bus Driver
30   Digging Potatoes
31   A Woman Called Faithless
32   Runaway
32   On First Looking into Raymond Chandler
33   Letter to Corn Island

Elizabeth Garrett
36   Rumaucourt

Fiona Hall
45   Sister Ev
46   Couple
46   Stopping the Breadman
47   Small Words
47   Pharaoh's Dream

Mimi Khalvati
48 Rubaiyat
49 The Poulterer
50 The Bowl
54 Baba Mostafa
55 Haiku

Linda Saunders
56 A Freethinker's Baptism
57 The Lepidopterist's Dream
58 Silences
58 Her Bed
59 Practice Board

Briar Wood
60 Fado
61 Aria
62 Moulding Heathcliff
63 The Bridal Feet
64 Falling Apart
65 Quite Like a Prayer

Adèle Geras
67 Needleworks

Jackie Kay
74 The Visit
76 The Telling Part
77 Bette Davis
77 Angela Davis
79 *From* Generations

S.J. Litherland
81 The Long Interval
82 The Wake
82 A Synagogue in Samarkand
85 The Debt Problem

Rachel Blake
86 The Pale Boy and the Old Woman
87 Transformations
88 Childhood Lane
89 Lifeline

Gwyneth Lewis
90   *From* Welsh Espionage
93   The Bad Shepherd
93   The Building Site
94   On Mayon Volcano
95   The Cut of Women's Clothes

Vuyelwa Carlin
96   The Dragon
97   Strange Dolls
97   The Drowned Girl
98   Monsters
99   Spring Fever
99   The Trees
100   Scots Pines
101   The Exile

Janet Fisher
102   Fifty Years On
103   But the difference
103   By the pump dry-eyed
104   Touching Up
104   Jocasta
105   Jonathan
105   Existentialist
106   Journey's End

Christine McNeill
107   Déjà vu
108   Close-up
108   Virus
109   'My daughter' *By a German Mother*
110   Geography Lesson
111   View from the Window
112   Direct Method
112   Drama
113   Viennese Remembrance
114   A Mystery

Angela Greene
115   Encounter
116   Cézanne
117   The Seal off Clogherhead

117   Recipe
118   Terrorist's Wife
119   Sand

Liz Cashdan
120   The Loggia
121   After School
121   To My Elder Brother
122   Cutting Loose
123   Mixed Singles
123   Deconstructions

Mary O'Donnell
124   Uncharted
125   Border Town
126   Histories
127   Cuckold
128   Mer-men, First-form
129   The Welcome House
130   Girl Warrior
131   Old Gardens Are Not Relevant

Katrina Porteous
133   If My Train Will Come
134   Factory Girl
135   Kicking Against the Walls
136   Ducks

Jill Maughan
137   Flames
138   A small death
139   Remembering
140   Long shadows

Tracey Herd
141   One of the Gang
142   After the Impossible Dream
143   In the Dark Museum
144   Treading Water
145   The Open Gate
146   Twilight on the River Cam
146   Grit and Snow

Christiania Whitehead
147   The unicorn is a symbol of virginity
148   From a Saxon monk to his love
149   Lindisfarne
150   Homily
151   Brutus' last song

Anne Rouse
152   Virginian Arcady
153   Round
153   Déjeuner sur l'herbe
154   Sacrificial Wolf
155   Row
155   Daytrip
156   England Nil
156   Her Retirement
157   Springfield, Virginia

Cynthia Fuller
158   Encounter
160   Cassandra
160   Pool
161   Beginning
162   Crossing the Edge
162   Self-centre

Lavinia Greenlaw
163   The Death of a Butcher
164   The Innocence of Radium
165   Hurting Small Animals
166   He wanted someone to cook chicken
166   Sex, Politics and Religion
167   The Chapel Snake
168   Anchorage
169   North
170   Off the Map
172   The Gift of Life

Introduction

A large number of the most interesting first collections offered to
Bloodaxe in the last year or so turned out to be by women poets.
Since Bloodaxe did not have the resources to publish even half of
them, Neil Astley decided that the best short-term solution would
be to bring out a fairly solid anthology. For some of the poets, this
would lead to eventual publication of a book-length collection. It
would enable those with smaller quantities of finished work to receive
a showing, and give them all some useful advance exposure.

Initially, the plan was to present about fifteen new poets, allowing
ten pages each, but as I read through all these unpublished first
collections the quality of the work convinced me that there was a
good argument for including more poets and being a little less gener-
ous with space. Having selected twenty, I then added a further five
whose collections we decided to solicit specifically for this anthology.
The resultant book is something of a hybrid – an anthology-cum-
introduction. It gives, I believe, a real sense of substance, but also
reflects the lively diversity that was such a pleasure to discover. Many
individuals are still solidly represented, in some cases by an entire
sequence (Elizabeth Garrett's fine 'Rumaucourt' cycle, for instance,
on page 36) and, where a poet has a wide range of approaches, by
a selection sufficient I hope to reflect this variety. The ordering of
each group has been decided by the poet concerned.

The necessity of selection is never a pleasant one. As usual, an
editor is oppressed by logistics, conscious of the limits beyond which,
by some unchallengable decree, the book is not allowed to grow.
The first criterion was that none of the poets should have previously
published a book, though pamphlets were acceptable. Then it
seemed important to convey a broad sense of what is going on *now*,
and not simply to give way to my predilections. However, I have
steered clear of "performance poetry", at least the kind that is
strongly dependent on the performer's personality, and so loses its
savour on the page. There are poets here whose work draws enrich-
ingly on the oral tradition – Jackie Kay's, for example – and is highly
perform*able*.

A significant point is that while all the poets represented are rela-
tive newcomers to publication, age was never the issue. Several are
under thirty, but many are a good deal older. All forms of discrimi-
nation in favour of the lower age-groups tend to discriminate against
women (award-funding bodies please note!): for a variety of well

documented reasons, our passage into a writing career is often belated, and rarely proceeds uninterrupted.

This brings me to the book's political implications. Though I am not aware of any ideological motives on the part of the publisher (it seems that the marketing of "women's writing" has moved away from specifically ideological thinking in recent years), the whole notion that women poets can legitimately be grouped together in this way, and that gender is almost a symbolic form of nationality, a line of cohesion and relationship whatever the superficial differences, owes everything to the Women's Movement, and the literary revolution it created. The very fact that such a book as this can be published at all proves the success of that revolution. It seems to me that any amassing of women's voices will necessarily amount to a fairly radical critique of current society. It is up to the reader to decide what this critique is, and if the poets are in fact united by any common characteristic bound up with gender. To me, the most striking impression is of heterogeneity, and if this is what readers see too, then perhaps it will have been one of the book's useful minor functions to show how many different kinds of poet a "woman poet" may actually be.

Poetry has changed a great deal over the last twenty years. The idea of its domination by a few "great" names (very largely male) still persists in some quarters, but is looking increasingly redundant. I believe that we have a process of democratisation on our hands, with women taking a major role in it, and that "more" has not in fact meant "worse", as the bleak old men of the right always assumed, but simply "various". The quality of much new writing testifies to the fact that poetry is increasingly being taught as a craft, not, sadly, to any great extent in the schools or universities, but in the numerous courses and workshops for adults that continue, fairly surprisingly, given the current political climate, to flourish. Of course, there are aspects of literary talent which cannot be taught, and craft, which can be, has its limits: poems written in the "workshop" may betray their origins by self-consciousness, or recognisable "tricks of the trade". Nevertheless, the awareness of poetry as an exacting apprenticeship which, at the same time, is open to everyone, seems to be a radically important development. Not so long ago, in the rush to throw out the idea of poetry as a club for the over-privileged, there was also a tendency to deny that it demanded anything much in the way of skill. Now, while the elite has been made to give at least some ground, notions of excellence, however broadly-based, have crept in at the grass-roots. It is no longer seen as malevolently patriarchal or excluding to ask of a poem that it sustains, as these poems do, the energy and integrity of its own structure.

Another fairly recent development has been the rise of the poetry competition, and the creation of a kind of competition-culture. It has many dubious and unpleasant characteristics: the restless search for the new name and literary flavour-of-the-month, leaving behind a trail of the apparently obsolete; the view of writing and writers as intensely individualistic, even combative, with no recognition of how much the most personal of poems is also part of the collective endeavour, and the inference that quality is instantly measurable and has a market-value. On the other hand, in a literary democracy emergence may be more difficult, and the competition can help to make at least a limited number of talents visible, while kindling a few gleams of public interest in poetry generally.

Several of the poets here have emerged in this way: Rachel Blake, Angela Greene and Mary O'Donnell were winners in the Bloodaxe National Poetry Competition, and Linda France, Fiona Hall, Jill Maughan, Katrina Porteous and Christiania Whitehead were major prizewinners in the *Evening Chronicle*'s annual competition in New-castle. Others have gained recognition by winning national literary awards: Lavinia Greenlaw, Gwyneth Lewis, Jill Maughan and Katrina Porteous are recent winners of the Society of Authors' Eric Gregory Awards (for promising poets under 30), while Angela Greene won Ireland's Patrick Kavanagh Award (given each year for an unpublished collection by a new writer). These poets would no doubt have emerged sooner or later anyway: winning a competition or an award simply sped the process. Furthermore, winning is always a great morale-booster. The part played in literary achievement by mere self-confidence has always been under-rated. And self-confidence is what, next to time, women have traditionally most lacked.

My wish for these poets is that they will go on being perceived as interesting long after they have ceased to be "new". New is one of the things that women poets in Britain are sanctioned to be. They can be funny, sexy, witty, rebellious and, perhaps, heartfelt – all fine as far as it goes, but I am not at all sure that even now, they are often perceived as having a full, authoritative poetic presence. Our senior women poets are dismally unhonoured, and many of the most accomplished writers of the older generations, from Sheila Wingfield to Anne Stevenson, have never had the recognition they deserve. Helen Dunmore suggests that there is a possible analogy with the way the establishment regards women priests. The patriarchs are reluctant to invest women with responsibilities not strictly quotidian.

Let them write biography...

Reading through the poems to be considered for this book, many of which revealed a deep interest in traditionally "female" subjects such as family relationships, and comparing them with some of the work by male poets recently published I began to wonder what had become of the "new man", that would-be endearingly vulnerable figure of the mid-eighties, whose apprenticeship to literature included the writing of sensitive poems about cooking (or was it eating?) ratatouille and changing the baby. Perhaps we only invented him. Now, it seems, a revised "new man" is abroad, one who is much more closely related to the old model. Even Bloodaxe, which publishes more women poets than any other British publisher, has several male poets on its list that I am tempted unkindly to include under the general heading The New Machismo – good poets, perhaps, but with a decided tendency to flex muscles and display tough-guy credentials. This, I think, is indicative of a widespread change of mood. The sub-text begins to suggest, as it did in the sixties, that real poets (and real lefties) are men. Could it be that women poets are again left holding the metaphorical babies?

Of course there is nothing wrong with holding babies but it should not be the only option. Women poets need, I think, to put up a special resistance to any urge they may have, or that is being foisted on them by others, to become the repositories of the finer feelings, the purveyors of a versified 'Body Shop' ethic. Related, perhaps to that queasy figure whom Virginia Woolf personified as the Angel in the House, and who tended to stay the hand of the woman reviewer just as she was about to write something juicily unflattering concerning a male author, this urge is no longer, God forbid, about pleasing men, but I wonder if it may be about flattering ourselves for being 'so much nicer than men'. Even if we were, niceness has very little to do with poetry. While women need not apologise for their human-interest poems, their love poems, their green poems, etc, and I do not apologise for including some of them here, I can't deny my pleasure at having found poets such as Eva Salzman and Janet Fisher prepared to talk authoritatively about motorways and jump-leads. The scientific and technical jargons can be extremely enriching for poetry, and it would be a pity if women were to go on feeling unnecessarily excluded from such energy-sources.

One of the most exciting things about this book is the variety of its dialects. Again, I cannot imagine that even a few years ago such variety would have emerged simply from a selection of current typescripts sent, mostly unsolicited, to a small English publisher. There are Irish, Welsh, Black-Scottish, New Zealand, South African, Austrian, Iranian and American poets here, chosen not for their nationality but for the freshness of their vision and vernacular. Even within small England, the voices are from areas as culturally distinct as Northumberland and the Sussex Coast.

The forms are correspondingly eclectic. There are poets such as Gwyneth Lewis who write in traditional rhyme and metre, others who are nearer to the unstructured rhythms of everyday speech, and a number who revel happily in the current stock of possibilities and seem as comfortable with the free-verse improvisation as the sestina. There may be no startling formal discoveries: what is new, I think, is the emergence of a kind of late twentieth-century urban dialect, a montage that reverberates with the noise, colour, slanginess, jargonising and information-glut of daily life. Briar Wood and Jackie Kay are its most obvious exemplars, but there are echoes of it in several others. Poetry's vital energies derive from the way we speak and it perhaps takes special courage for women poets to write in a way that stresses this relationship, rather than seek approval by flaunting their more academic literary credentials.

The feminist consciousness that might once have been self-searching now often takes a more outward-looking stance. A kind of sardonic generosity permeates many of the poems about men, for example, Anne Rouse's elegy, 'Sacrificial Wolf' (page 154) and Linda France's 'Bus Driver' (page 30): *'By, he could tell some tales – / the busfulls of women / who don't get enough. Joe fancies / a poem for him and his bus. / This is it. No frills.'* Joe is not allowed to get away with anything, although he gets his poem; teasing, unthreatened, the writer confronts Joe's sexism with gentle parody rather than hate. Not all the views of heterosexual communications are so optimistic: Tracey Herd, for example, rewrites the Cinderella story to end with the heroine slashing her wrists, 'having played the glass slipper game / to the very end' ('After the Impossible Dream', page 142). Pain and rage are certainly present in this volume: so too are physical celebration and *jouissance* – in both senses of the word. Women's love poetry is in general much sexier than men's. An ancient vein of Christian erotic mysticism is explored by Christiania Whitehead: I find her poetry strange and difficult but quite unlike anything else I have encountered. Often there is a great sense of men being observed – whether as fathers, lovers, brothers or, indeed, bus drivers. Women poets, it seems, are behaving more like novelists these days, and are perhaps putting some of them in the shade with their patient, unjudging observation of male characters and character.

Though no longer the preoccupation it was in the seventies, the reclamation of the "silenced woman" of the past continues among many of these writers. She may be the unknown inventor of the recipe for drop biscuits in Angela Greene's "found poem" (page 117) who talks to us so plainly and touchingly across the centuries, or, more likely, she is a longed-for mother or grandmother. Perhaps it would be fitting to end this introduction to a book that celebrates the new by quoting from Mimi Khalvati's 'Rubaiyat' (page 49), a poem to her Persian grandmother. It might have merely been a clever pastiche of Edward Fitzgerald's *Omar Khayyam*. Somehow, Khalvati has breathed her own life and vision into the stately, Victorian iambs. It is a more emotional poem than most Englishmen and many English women would dare to write, but I challenge any honest reader to be unmoved by it:

> My grandmother would rise and take my arm,
> then sifting through the petals in her palm,
> would place in mine the whitest of them all:
> 'Salaam, dokhtaré-mahé-man, salaam!'
>
> 'Salaam, my daughter-lovely-as-the-moon!'
> Would that the world could see men, Telajune,
> through your eyes! Or that I could see a world
> that takes such care to tend what fades so soon.

CAROL RUMENS

Eva Salzman

CLAUDIA RICHARDSON

Acknowledgements: *Poetry Review* and *Foolscap*.

EVA SALZMAN was born in 1960 in New York City, and grew up in Brooklyn where – from the age of 10 until 22 – she was a dancer, and later a choreographer. She was educated at Bennington College, Vermont, and took an MFA in poetry at Columbia University. She moved to Britain in 1985, did some sporadic teaching of dance and exercise, and then set up her present "cottage industry" – an out-of-print book search-service which she runs from her home in Brighton.

Her poems have appeared in various magazines and anthologies, and she was one of the writers featured in *Poetry Review*'s 'New British Poets' special issue in 1987. Her first collection, *The English Earthquake*, is forthcoming from Bloodaxe Books. ●

The English Earthquake

Somewhere, a cup tinkles in its saucer.
A meek 'oh my' passes down the miles
of manicured gardens, as armies rumble

the monuments of cities, continents away.
The budgie chirps 'goodness' to thin air
while Bach quivers slightly and the fat roast

sways in the oven, brain-dead, but chuckling
in its oil. Such a surprise: the settling ground,
innocent with rape and mustard, groaning

under its weight of roses. The premier
sees stars, plumps her pillows for photographs.
Alas, *Watchtower* faces are falling as life goes on

and the Ex-Major winds back years to the war
– its incendiary thrill – his wife flushed
with disbelief as the earth moves unexpectedly,

the giant baby at the core of the planet
rocking its apocalyptic cradle
gently, wailing: 'Hungry, hungry, hungry'.

Ending up in Kent

I'm leaning out the cottage window, latch
unfastened, trying to see for miles, further.
Postcard-picture me in a country of thatch,
twisted lanes, daub and wattle. I entertain
with coal-fires and gas cylinders.
For all through the year it rains, I freeze.
The neighbouring oasts are like spindles,
fat with the wound-up thread of absent summer.
I walk detergent streams, in search of trees.

Someone's put me in a story-book, but kills
every tree before my entrance.
I follow an ordnance map and find
frightening rows of straight and vacant pines.
The earth as barren as the rugs
people in my nearby town put down. Medicine
sting of pine. Listen there, hear nothing. No bird sings.
I'm told that insects are the only living things
in that Forestry Commission flat. And slugs.

Gala-day on the Tonbridge-Hastings line
and my landlord's chopping down his chestnut trees.
Two train stops and you're at a famous waters place
where they renovate shops into postcard prints.
Inside are offices, outside a show of wealth. In me,
when I walk that scenic, cobbled walk, a tall tree
grows crooked, like a money-graph
zigzagging into civic failure. In warm weather
they sell sulphur from the Wells for your pleasure.
Good Health! November and the Guy will burn.
What leaves are left on what trees are left will turn.

With Steve Ovett in Preston Park

Man makes his spirit strong by lifting weights.
His endurance is beyond belief; he swims channels,
plays rugby, clambers to the North Pole
because it's there (not here) and chugs
along for miles on his own two legs
with *Rocky* playing in his ear. Hooray!

This statue should inspire us all –
this Brighton man, built of bronze (hard work
has made him) and he pants heroically,
striving, though he's frozen on his pedestal
at the high point of an endless marathon.
Note the artistic strain, the spare frame
with the sinews moulded in overdrive. If he's hollow-
eyed and starving, like a refugee, it's because
the sculptor grew confused along the way.

Joggers of flesh-and-blood pound by on the peace-mile
circuit, in rain or sleet or snow; the will
of man is priceless, artless. Seasons pass
and roses at his feet die back, are pruned,
shoot up again while green corrosive streaks inch down
the cheeks, oxidisation like a macabre sweat;
he's running as hard as he can away from his maker.

Rain in New York

The magic holds.
A siren sounds.
Oily water runs in the gutters
and you walk through rainbows.
Mica chips fizz underfoot
– you want to scoop them out from the stone –

and traffic lights like totem-poles
reflect in glass streets.
The residents, not beautiful, are also slick,
test you out,
talk sex and big
and best, bop across the wet road
and take, three steps at a skip
the sooty stairs down into the subway hole.

Gladiatorial cabbies have it out.
I'm running maybe to see the fire.
Quick, I get in one that says 'For Hire',
ask for the Brooklyn Bridge.
He goes 'Why not?'
Then, racing Angels down the avenue
he turns, says 'Jesus,
the weather's lousy. How's it with you?
Jeez, crime is terrible these days.
The bastards, they should be shot.'

I'd had a mind to ask a stranger back,
but it was someone else's mind put on by mistake.
Something was burning, but what?
Now I speed down Broadway alone
spinning it out on a run of green
while the rain pours down, sparky,
hurtling past Dave's towards Chambers Street,
splashing red and amber lights like eyes,
the prides of yellow, prowling beasts

I've left behind in my ordinary taxi.
And past the denizens all on heat,
kohl-eyed and carnival-studded,
stunning and striding
like giants onto the dancing floor in my head,
glamorous and vain,
the glitter floating in their hair – they're stars –
and sequins on their dress, like rain.

Cheap Thrills

Picture me as a heroine from some lurid rag,
clothes disarranged,
half-off
following an unceasing flow of adventures
all guaranteed to make your heart beat hard.
Pirates accost me
while I appear unwilling,
but luck rains down on me
at 'The End'
in the form of a hero who hammers lust
into the routine halo.
The tale is completed
with a man and woman glued together
only because your invitation has expired
on that final page
where the words wind up the romance.

Picture me
as a leading lady. It's time,
made-up,
to go out, see friends, take too much drink,
then find the best way to go home
alone. There were so many partners
at the dance, the time I had was fantastic.
Heading back, a man on the train has eyes
for me, I for him.
For a lark,
we indulge in a love-affair
from Fourteenth
Street to Forty-Second
where one of us finally calls it off,
disembarks. At home, the dog
all this time has been sober, left to her own
society, my book open nearby
to the same page too many days running.
Clothes lie
where I left them, trickling out
from under the bed, messily dressing
the chairs, the room. Still desperately

in love with some stranger, I sleep in fits
and starts,
dreaming of the most impossible things.

Horoscope

Authority is the order of the day. Don't be deterred by
well-meaning warnings. Last minute changes could astound you.
Stick to your guns and be very clear about your position.
ASTROLOGY NOW MAGAZINE

Thanks a million, oh revolving stars
and your spokesmen who must make cant
of the unknown: advice like hourglass sand
through fingers. Still I look to the Taurus bull
in the *Evening Standard* to learn to be hopeful.
But if 'Stop' signs sounded like this I'd be dead.
My cusp, the ram, also has horns and a butting head,
alas, bleats circular phrases too, vague things
like the future. I discover how a president
consults his chart for our forecast. A lucky star?
Heaven help us! Precisely, the astrologer says as she rings
her hot-line to find the astral positions on war.

Birds Courting Loudly

The birds' twittering fuss kept me awake
half the night it seemed. 'Available' they tweet
and chatter, and with their plumage make
their boasts. I wished their mating were more discreet
and subtle, allowing me to sleep,
conducted more like a hush-hush affair

and less in the manner of some tabloid
with a Page 3 photo of a lady, bare
from the waist up and grinning like she's selling
washing soap. So much for the quietude
of the country. Worse than the siren's wail
or monotonous rumble of traffic over a bridge
are these birds advertising for a male
or scrambling for a female with whom to pledge
their bird-troth – however short or long
that lasts. Late morning comes and I forgive
them their clamour, the pronunciation of a song
for some raw, nature-perfect love I'll never sing
with honesty (religionless, unprincipled, not rare)
or accuracy, as long as I may live.

Soliloquy

I'm thinking about how ordinary this day is
except that I know my neighbour's giving birth.
If we didn't know, we'd simply say it's sunny
and let's hope it stays that way for the play
we plan this evening. Last night through the wall
at one I heard their privacy – voices, low
and purposeful, a shifting. But all I really knew
was a crying fox outside the window. Then a dog
howling at it, then more dogs across the field.
Curtains glow with headlights, are dark again
when they've gone. Silence settles back. I lie awake.

Great pain is somewhere else, but today the clock
ticks placidly and the dog yawns. No fox screams
in the daylight. A lone bird suddenly trills at ten.
Is it now? I think. But the signs of nature
do not reflect our solipsistic world. At dusk
the players will gather behind the castle ruins,
well-rehearsed and ready, with the audience
assembled in rows, the programmes rustling.
We've already read the play, yet eagerly
we wait to be shown the effortless work. The play begins.

Time Out

Imagine there being no exacting word for time,
there being nothing to waste or save, invent
or slip away. Then who would fight the crime
of its fast passing? I'd take, say, the three-cigarette

train departing half-past-after-the-last-word
which wants saying (and not a moment too soon!)
while the numberless dial of my watch would refer
to a changing mise-en-scène winding from sun to moon,

or some event to an eventual end, when a black 'For Hire'
drives me home on its own good time. *Good* time. For tides
aren't for living by, but are only there to admire
occasionally on trips to the timeless sea-sides.

Nor do we milk cows, farm a natural time, say to friends:
'I'll meet you at the end of this cooking of rice'
or, more vaguely still: 'You know...when the afternoon ends.'
When? Would I be on time, guided by a smoky feel of night,

when it fell, in my bones – another made-up clocking-in machine?
But how would I measure these purposeful distances run,
or almost run, as the case would more likely seem?
The racers might just laugh or chat at the starting-gun.

Yet I wouldn't think to worry if I were late
for anything, wouldn't care by when which boat
came in. Stockbrokers would forget the date
and leisurely ask if you had the 'time', as a joke.

Some joke, infernal time! Not a word, not well-made policy,
but some black jester's dressed-up devastating game
which lets me put off the proverbial plot, infinitely,
so I could wait here forever before you finally came, or not.

Power Games

The traffic eyes went blank with cataracts,
lorries buckled, the rigid aerial spines
bent for mutant coats – Uri Geller with a blank cheque.

The ant-column of cars wayward and drunk,
all the toy streets had wound down to crime
and accidents, the shops and offices funked.

At home, the TV sizzling like bacon
we were rehearsing 'I love you' in pantomime
– difficult words for the practised pagan.

Think, that very day we juggled jump-lead cables,
bewildered by the dead car, those precarious lines
we were examining for plus and minus labels.

One false move, those red and blue aortas
could shock you the other side of 'live', if misaligned
– the right key, the booby-trapped mortice.

We fell into the pub, sat comfortable in the dark
under currentless bulbs with lame plugs, sipping wine,
negotiating the odd, casual remark.

Then you broke the triangle with that effective,
skilful shot; but the white flew off the table
as all at once the mains switched on to that collective
'Ah', as if this were first light, the start of time.

Linda France

LINDA FRANCE was born in 1958 in Newcastle. After living in Dorset, Leeds, London and Amsterdam, she returned to the North East in 1981 to live in the North Tyne valley. She has two children and works as a part-time tutor in adult education. In 1988 she won the Basil Bunting Award in the Newcastle *Evening Chronicle* Poetry Competition with her long poem *Acts of Love*, later published as a pamphlet by the Echo Room Press, and in 1990 won the Basil Bunting Award again. For the 1989 Hexham Abbey Festival she wrote and appeared in a poetry and music collaboration, *Fire and Brimstone*, based on the life of the artist John Martin. Her first book-length collection is forthcoming from Bloodaxe. ●

Acknowledgements: *Evening Chronicle* (Newcastle), *The North, The Rialto, The Wide Skirt* and *Writing Women*.

If Love Was Jazz

If love was jazz,
I'd be dazzled
By its razzmatazz.

If love was a sax,
I'd melt in its brassy flame
Like wax.

If love was a guitar,
I'd pluck its six strings,
Eight to the bar.

If love was a trombone,
I'd feel its slow
Slide, right down my backbone.

If love was a drum,
I'd be caught in its snare,
Kept under its thumb.

If love was a trumpet,
I'd blow it.

If love was jazz,
I'd sing its praises,
Like Larkin has.

But love isn't jazz.
It's an organ recital.
Eminently worthy,
Not nearly as vital.

If love was jazz,
I'd always want more.
I'd be a regular
On that smoky dance-floor.

Hennaing My Hair

A man I know brought me henna
from the Souk in Marrakech.
The old Moroccan apothecary creased his eyes,
offered a love potion of crushed insects.
My friend only took the henna, so he says,
a plump parcel of foreign khaki powder.

It seems as if Mrs Grieve doesn't approve
of such unashamed exotica –
only the shortest of entries in her *Modern Herbal* –
'Other names: Mehndi, Al-Khanna,
Jamaica Mignonette' – a harem herb,
for female adornment, pleasure.

I mix the henna, with hot water,
to a thick spinachy mud,
spread it on my head, recklessly.
Wet brown clods splatter sink, floor,
me. The whole morning I'm turbaned,
irresistibly aware of my hair, alchemy.

After four heady hours, I rinse it off,
the provocative sculpture my hair's become.
It takes more water than they see a month
in Marrakech to wash it clean,
to shampoo out the last grainy residue.
The suds foam ochre.

I towel hair I think's returned to normal
but, as it dries, my forehead's wisped
with curling copper filaments;
my head's on fire, brazenly aflame,
a red as wild, as cunning
as a vixen on heat.

Better, I think, than aphrodisiacs.

Elementary
(for Rufus)

I ask my son what he knows of earth,
of properties of metal,
the rings in the heart of wood,
what shapes he can trace in air,
how deep is the blue of water;
remind him to take care with fire.

He has a dangerous fondness for fire,
my son, learning the lessons of earth;
knows magnets are science, metal,
observes their attraction through water.
He's aware that a kite, and he, needs air,
the paper he'd miss so much is wood.

We scramble hand in hand through the wood
near our house, feeling the damp earth
spring under our feet, the lapping of water
in the silence. The cold air
makes him cough so we go home to the fire,
welcomed by kettle's singing metal.

His toys are plastic; mine were metal,
with sharp corners. They rusted in water.
Now the fashion's back for wood,
carved and painted trains, trucks and fire-
engines. Things have changed. This earth
I thought I knew, and love, is mutable as air.

My son was four the year the air
blew from the east, poisoned by fire,
a fire kindled with no wood.
The smell of my sweat was metal.
We couldn't trust rain, milk or earth,
were afraid to drink the water.

He loves to play in water,
and I to watch him, in the tenuous air
of summers. I lean against knotted wood,
by the river glinting metal.
As certain as flames in fire
we're held in the breath of earth.

I pray to the gods of air, goddesses of wood
and water, that he'll be saved from fire,
and save, like precious metal, all he knows of earth.

Gate-crasher

She smiles like Sheba, says her name's a gift.
Mother thinks she's catching up on homework.

Her wide mouth freezes as the party hots up,
when they remove the syringe's red cap,

when they ease the needle into her arm,
when the white boys shoot her

full of smack.

An orange sliver of moon drips citrus;
Catherine-wheels spin inside her throat.

A seventeen-year-young roller-coaster
hurtling; blur of policemen, nurses, her mother

who named her.

Back at school she's a star for a week or two.
The prick in her arm heals; not the voodoo nightmare,

her unasked-for gift, lies.

Bus Driver

He has some crack for everyone,
has Joe – transporting his cargo
across the high seas of the shire.
All of *us* are female,
but *he's* at the helm, our figurehead.

His blue and white bus is all red
inside. The effect abattoir, or womb –
appropriate for transition, from A to B.
For Joe, it's A to bloody B
and back again four times daily.
He gave up smoking, couldn't stick it.

My funny hat confuses him. He's curious.
Over the jutting back of seats, we chat.
'Where's the money in poems?'
he replies, when I confess I write.
'A Jackie Collins. That's what they want.
Fantasy. Romance.' Joe knows.

By, he could tell some tales –
the busfulls of women
who don't get enough. Joe fancies
a poem for him, and his bus.
This is it. No frills.

Digging Potatoes

Enter said the blush of wine,
Rosehip candlelight.
Continue said my eyes,
As you made love to me
From the other side of the room.

In the darkness of the car
You dazzled me, like headlights,
And made me shiver,
As if I needed some choke.

What could I do but give you
Potatoes and no promises;
And tell you now that the flower
Down from the mill, by the river's edge,
You thought might be agrimony –
Its name is yellow loosestrife.

That's what I wish for you:
No troubles;
Only the sound of water
Nearby, and potatoes.

A Woman Called Faithless

There's a woman called Faithless
living in my house.

She moves from room to room,
trailing musk and ambergris.

Mouth parted, faintly bruised,
she is moody as seaweed. Her glad

gull's eye collects shells, bones.
Her favourite haunt is horizontal.

A creature wearing only a necklace
of names, she is all things to all men.

You can count on her to kiss and tell.
I think she's a swan on holiday:

fascinating from across a lake;
all beak and hissing when you get close.

I watch her giving the Man of the House
the largest slice of cake. I know her

too well; I cannot trust her.
She's Faithless, as a cat;

steals love from cupboards.

Runaway

It was dark when we came home,
door still jammed as if she'd shut it
behind her, covered her tracks.
A cold black doglessness.

It's hard to say what I missed most:
waggish ears; her casual furstyle;
polished eyes under politician's brows;
her Guinness jig; tabor of her tail;
or that bark I could pick out
a bone's throw from Battersea Dog's Home.

But nothing. Nothing but a flat tangle
of straw, a half-eaten dish of Poacher's.
We spent all evening not talking about dogs,
seeming to listen to the jazz on Radio 3,
tuned in to the wind growling at the curtains.

Midnight kept us awake
till a small canine voice called
to us to open the door, like a teenage son
who'd forgotten his key. She was pure skulk
until she remembered she was our best friend.
And that was what her tongue was for.

On First Looking into Raymond Chandler

Of course I always knew who you were. I
grew up with Humphrey Bogart, Hollywood.
I used to think everyone talked that good.
Then, browsing a second-hand bookstall, I
saw this faded green and cream Penguin. Five
pence, the man said. For Church funds. I handed
it over, took you home to read in bed.
Some nightcap. The only place I went was wide-
awake, dreaming of California,

where the high-life's pretty low and the heat
shimmers like your prose. I could feel it all,
cool as anything, on the rocks, or neat.
Now your hero's mine too, and you can call
anytime and find me right on your beat.

Letter to Corn Island
4 November 1988

I

Your letter took only nineteen days
to reach me. Nineteen days.
Over four thousand miles.
I looked it up – a small blue
ice-cream-cone-shaped speck
on page 89 of the *Reader's Digest*
Great World Atlas:
'Is. del Maiz (Nic. & U.S.)'

Your yellow paper
smelled of Caribbean sun
and your blue ink deep as the sea.

It's sunny here too –
a glassy sun, pretending
to be warmer than it is.
Crystal days, hard and sharp;
nights cold as opal
(but maybe you've forgotten)
and the always surprising
whiteness of mornings
that last all day in the shade.

II

Those shells you sent
before (my New Year gift)
sit on the stair-head window-sill.

I see them every day.
The Bougainvillaea flowers are faded,
their carnival pink
leaching into earthy English brown.
The window's draught scattered them,
chameleon skins round the room.
That, and their fading, made you feel
further away, longer.

III

        I need to ask
how a road looks when it ends,
the best way to crack a sea almond,
and what happens in a hurricane?
(They called it Joan on the radio.
I'm trying to imagine you
not letting her blow you away.)

        Castaway on Corn Island –
diving from canoes into clear water
past coral 'trees of stone',
anemones and rainbow fish winking
from pirate wrecks.
(Today I pulled up the nasturtiums,
translucent withered skeins
from last night's frost.)
And listening to the locals talk
of their fishing and smuggling,
someone else's war, as you eat
lobster you caught yourself
and cooked with breadfruit, coconut milk.
(Today I baked our first mince pies
and Walter Gabriel died in his sleep.)

IV

        It's really much the same here –
another autumn burning itself out.
The children are a year bigger,
growing into themselves.

        And tomorrow's Bonfire Night.
I'll watch the silver showers

streak the sky's black
and turn it all upside down
and see coral reefs and you, diving.

V

Your letter on yellow paper
seems different from the rest.
There are no empty spaces,
no white ghosts between the words.
And each word is louder,
certain of its place.
You say you're happy now '(first time)'.

But you'll be home
for Christmas and we can sit
by my stove and, over mugs of tea,
share our years, grain by grain.
Then I'll feel, like now,
the gritty ache of missing you.

Elizabeth Garrett

Acknowledgements: *New Poetry from Oxford 2* (1984)

ELIZABETH GARRETT was born in 1958 in London, and grew up in the Channel Islands. Since completing her D.Phil. at Oxford University on the Fool in modern English and French poetry , she has worked in the Bodleian Library and is currently employed by the Voltaire Foundation.

Her poems have appeared in various magazines and anthologies, and she was one of the writers featured in *Poetry Review*'s 'New British Poets' special issue in 1987. A pamphlet selection of her poetry, *The Mortal Light*, was published by the Mandeville Press in 1990. Her first book-length collection is forthcoming from Bloodaxe Books. ●

Rumaucourt
(for my father)

> *Memory believes before knowing remembers*
> WILLIAM FAULKNER

Close-up

An accident of memory reversed.
Red I can see; a lens tensed
To contain the spread of a whelming blur.
I adjust the view: the mass contracts and breathes.
Lub-dubbing its crimson life, a geranium heaves
Into focus, here, hot with the throb and thrum
Of a heart, pulsing beneath my thumb.

I.

Rumaucourt, 1937

His window opened onto monochrome.
Things were simpler then, in black and white,
He said: the clock's hands governed by the rhythm
Of the farm, the tocsin of the cockerel,
Soft alarm of clinking chains, and cattle
Restive in the barn. I tried to see
His point. I saw the cows were black and white,
But were they really Friesian? And had the kitchen
Clock stuck stubbornly at three,
Or did it ever chime? And had night fallen
Early there – or did the camera lie?

Josianne

After-dinner faces cloud the kitchen;
Empty glasses. Hands forever reaching
For the bottle. A small beribboned child
Muzzles her snarling brother with a sieve.
She holds her audience captive as she smiles
For the box. They say it never lies,
Arrests its image, holds the captor hostage.

Andrée

Home-maker, child-bearer, wife
And servant, mistress of grief.
Habit mocked her with 'Mother'
Though she just subsists, neither
Possessed nor quite possessing,
Set back from her brood, guessing
At their fledgling schemes to fly

The nest, or cuckoo-greedy,
Squeeze her from the hearth she warmed
With her own womb, burning, torn
From her now. She stands detached,
Not quite managing to touch
Her husband's shoulder. The gap
Is framed, fixed, in white and black.

Robert

Here is a man who shares my father's blood,
But not his name. I ponder that.
Who measured out the portions? Were they fair,
Or did this stranger get the better share?
I'd have to dig below the skin to where
The stuff shunts breathlessly its red load
Through the tunnelled flesh, to find the answer.

Not here. Not now. He lives another tense.
The chair-back takes the burden of his laughter
Silently. He's looking at his daughter;
Feels her pull and loves the way she winds him
Round her little finger. Does he sense
His wife behind him?

Sons. Les Sons. Les Sens

Guillaume, Yves, Arsène. Roll the strange
New tastes across your tongue, mouthing a child's
Vague grace before a meal: E oh me, Amen.
Spell me a face for each name. I'm reading through
You squinting one-eyed through a Glacier Mint
Sucked smooth as a camera's lens. There are two
Men amused by a muzzled boy. Recall again
My cousins, much removed: Guillaume, Yves, Arsène.

The Go-Between

Close the book and fold them into dark.
Now tell me why a one-eyed world goes flat
And how I should measure absence with a look
And how I might cover distance with my hand
And how I should trace my blood in white and black.
Close your eyes; shrink down behind my lens.
Now show me where day begins, night ends.

II.

First Light

When first we woke in that place, we may have sensed
Our own desertion there,
Lying in the high room, in the too high bed,
Searching the light as it edged on the window-sill
Too slowly, and eight flies in aimless quadrille
Troubled the tall air.

At cock-crow, memory crept back like a truant lover
Mocking our wise fear
Of the stiff furniture, the dust cover
Of sleep, till we longed to abandon what we'd become
Beneath sleep in that strange bed and abandoned room
Waiting for light to appear.

We are ourselves and more, waking to what
We've come for; finding more
Than we want or can ever push back, like the slow light
On the window-sill, the heavy sheets, the air,
The importunate tug of the blood, our being here
Waking to Rumaucourt.

The Kitchen

Soft shift of air in milky somnolence;
Stir, but do not wake.
I finger-coax the door; obedient
Somnambulist returning to its frame.
A sour lactic sweetness trails a foam
Of bubbles in its wake.

Nothing's greatly changed. The table charts
An archipelago
Of wine-stains. Coral atolls, skerries, scars
Of civilisation in the woodgrain sea.
A ghosted clockface haunts the wall at three,
Mocked by its shifting shadow.

Their faces ghost elsewhere; but someone's left
His smile in a glass
Beside the sink. The loving bubbles cling
Where, white and pink, a plaster rictus drifts
In mute suspense: smothered laughter doubling
His collapsed lips' loss.

When sourmouthed morning comes, he'll find them both –
The laughter and the loss –
Swallowing grief with the inward gasp of mirth,
Putting senescence in its place, teeth
In theirs, hiding pointless truth beneath
The necessary false.

Beneath the door, a strand of strawlight slipping
Dawn's drawn lot.
She'll try to sweep it out, the woman sleeping
Cruelly bare without her body's apron
Bundled here, neat, far from the undone
Flesh, its careful knot.

Thresholds

Loosed in the yard like gangaboon hens, to grub
For treasure sunk in mud;
Flouting *défense de, verboten, forbidden,* we robbed
Decay of its blistered carapace, breaking the crust
In greed for communion: crumbs in our hands and rust
In our mouths, like the taste of blood.

Swung by day from disastered beams, swung
Above splintered kingdoms of straw,
Tossed like chaff through asthmatic half-light, spun
Into darkness, drunk on parabola, high in the crooked
Rafters' cage, stalling the ripcord, hooked
On the lapse of the backward yaw.

Then hunger gnawed. Rats among the rafters
Drove us from the barn
Towards the tense meniscus of their laughter:
Trembling at the window's lucid brink,
Between their bubble and the blackness, shrink
Or burst, worlds turned.

That night we ate off plates despair had laid
Deep in the beaten earth
Against the pulsing forces as they ploughed
The Flemish trench. For years the coulter chucked
Up shards, yet some survived, wise to the shock
Of grit between our teeth.

What threshold we had crossed to reach the coils
Of curdled light that wound
Us in, we did not ask; nor why the spoiled
Supper lay stonecold in Andrée's place
Beside the fire, nor why her dumb face
Cried tears down.

Second Light

In sleep, voiceless, calling out for water
In a strange tongue,
Not mine, she came, as if to her own daughter,
Spilling silver droplets on the floor
Beside my bed, her hand, trembling where
The chill glass hung.

Darkness slid across my tongue, the taste
Of earth, cold, aching
Down my throat. A cut geranium laced
Through her nightgown's trellis, shivered towards the breeze
Where soldiers lay beneath their sodden wreaths
Of poppies, beyond waking.

It sprung at the prying tip of each knife flicked
By Arsène in the barn:
Scattering rats across the beams he'd pick
Them off like flies, till there was nothing left
To kill, and boredom on its belly crept
Away from the empty farm.

It wilted in a vase beside her bed,
Sick, the spoiled daughter
With her baby, crying like a child
For her mother, only now, to come and take
The shameful thing away. I woke,
Crying out for water.

The Window

Small rain; the slow crow drawl
Across fields to where
Distance hangs like a net curtain drawn
Against knowing. Irksome blankness, me blinking
The mote from my eye, and the fly-speck inching
The grey mesh of air.

To push this thing aside, throw wide the sky's
Window, breast the jutting
Cloud-sill and transcribe land's ancient lie,
From scattered reams of fields, tracing the cursive
Signature of contour, road, and river,
Clear beyond doubting.

Mist rolls in like a sudden sea; my name
Wades through my breath –
Glass clouds if you look too close or hard –
Each finger traces a path to the same yard,
The same six hens fretting the dumb
Palimpsest of earth.

III.

The Betrayal

Turning another page, I felt time leap
A ragged breach, the heart tricked out of a beat
That lasted twenty years. Colour spilled
Across the page like a bad mistake, spoiled
The bib and tucker ways of black and white,
And caught me there, betraying my ignorance
Like a zip undone: the dumb innocence
Of a smile as easy as a camera's parting
Gesture, gift of a Medusa, thwarting
The hand's escape, the trapped bird's flight.

Looking across my shoulder at their faces
Now, their buckled smiles and our neat cases
On the doorstep, Andrée's halfway hand
And her eternal hanky, I understand
The true and hopeless sense of *Au revoir*
As they had meant it. Their appeal with our
Unkind parole vouchsafed: *Au r'voir – au r'voir.*
Still, *she* kept her word, for in the utter
Silence of this frame, her fingers flutter
Still: *l'adieu suprême des mouchoirs.*

The Return

A child's geography. If nothing moved
Or altered, I might sense the dark way back
Through corridors of poplars where the louvred
Air breathes balsam; past the girl in black
Beside the cemetery, two chickens dangling
By the legs from either hand; the rabid
Dog after its tail; the voices wrangling
Over cattle prices, and the dazed
Beasts waiting; past the yellow mitten
Waving from the fence – *tout droit!* until
The gate, the yard, the window where I'd written
Names, all welcomed my return.
                                        And still
I'm on the outside looking in. *Ouvres-moi*
Ta porte pour que je puisse te revoir.

                    *   *   *

Douai, Cambrai, Écourt, Rumaucourt.
It is not names that change or disappear,
But faces and their features, like a rumour
Tongues and time pull out of shape. Here
I can turn my back on the unanswered door,
Knowing who stands behind, my hand light
On the latch to lift and open, ready to show
Me round, knowing my way in, as out,
By heart, a journey of the blood, the slow
Footfall of diastole and systole through the night.

                    *   *   *

Turning back, I leave things as I found them:
Place in its pot the bright geranium,
By the door in a yard at the heart of Rumaucourt,
Between Douai, Cambrai, the Pas de Calais and the Nord,
In the crease of a map scuffed blank by endless folding.

Only the map of the blood I'll keep, to tuck
In here, and here; the spacious holdings
Of the head; the heart's soft ruck.

Fiona Hall

FRASER ROBINSON

Acknowledgements: *Evening Chronicle* (Newcastle) and *The Rialto*

FIONA HALL was born in 1955 in Swinton, Manchester. After reading French at Oxford, she qualified as a First School teacher and taught in a squatter settlement in Gaborone, Botswana. More recently, she has worked as a teacher and playgroup leader in north Northumberland where she now lives with her two daughters.

Her poems have appeared in various magazines, and in 1988 she won the Edward Boyle Prize in the Newcastle *Evening Chronicle* Poetry Competition. She did not write anything until she was 30: 'My poems seem to come out of moments of intensified awareness, from a sudden acute consciousness of how things really are. It took me years to realise that I could try to express in words this feeling almost of pain that I recognised in other people through their writing and music.' ●

Sister Ev

She was my aunt, long dead when I was born;
I called her as my dad did, 'Sister Ev'.
Her name was used to remonstrate and warn:
Eat up, you'll get TB like Sister Ev,

You've Sister Ev's sharp tongue. At least
the sour old maid was one I'd never meet,
until brown photographs among her creased
brown letters smoothed, to mirrors, at my feet.

You're reading here, tight-lipped, hair back; but there,
a rippling mane cascades – it won a prize.
There must have been some man who breathed *That hair!*
to you, lust steadying in his eyes,

So what went wrong? It isn't hard to guess –
you spent your youth on bringing up your brothers.
Your lemon-flavoured words I reassess
as pith, which, like your hair, now taunts in others.

Couple

Something from the first in the way
you watched his face and would tend
to stand very close said *not just
good friends.*

Next time you both wore rings.
Your eyes were locked so fast
crowds couldn't push between.
Would it last?

Older now, you sit some feet apart,
suffering writer's doubt in isolation.
You walk the collies during the day. *He* seeks
promotion.

Some things you know he'll never understand
(however much you drag him off to Culture),
but work back North soon cleared your head on where
you'd stay in future.

You've kept the bed you made, content beyond
the lurid dreams of those who would condemn
a steadfastly domestic Cheltenham couple
for being men.

Stopping the Breadman

*I think that I have failed to stop
my breadman leaving bread.* So it is
with your note in my hand that
I wait for his van, which is where
we began years ago when I spoke
to your husband with bread
in his hand: *I think that I
have failed to stop the breadman.*
Bread days in hundreds have passed on and
the breadman is still leaving bread and
I think that I have failed to stop

what began years ago when I spoke
to your husband; which is why
you have gone,
                        failing to stop the bread.

Small Words

You will complain
I was intrusive:
no more than your hands.

I read your card
to her, small words:
you wrote *all my love*.

Pharaoh's Dream
(BBC TV, 27 November 1989)

At one o'clock it was the thin cattle,
dun beasts against a parchment plain.
God help the spindle-legged calves
that comfort-sucked at wrinkled leather udders;
the prickly pear was finished, air
all that was left to blow out skins like bladders.

At two o'clock it was the fat beasts,
grey-coated store-cattle digesting
a bellyful of lunch in their green pasture.
Hear, Hear, they lowed. Ears twitched,
flicked off the flies of rumour,
settled: famine talk was not in order.

Much more than a thousand miles apart,
the herds stand to. It was his dream
that thin ate fat. Awake, he sees
they die, apart; for no road runs between.

Mimi Khalvati

MIMI KHALVATI was born in 1944 in Tehran. She trained at Drama Centre, London, has worked in the UK and in Iran as an actor and director, and now lives in London with her two children. Her poems have been published in magazines including *Artrage*, *The North*, *PN Review*, *Poetry Review*, *Writing Ulster* and *Writing Women*. In 1989 she was co-winner of the Poetry Business Competition with her pamphlet collection *Persian Miniatures* (Smith/Doorstop, 1990), and was joint winner of the 1990 Peterloo Poets Poetry Competition Afro-Caribbean/Asian prize. Selections of her poems appear in *New Voices* (Anvil Press, 1990) and *Camden Voices* (Katabasis, 1990). ●

Acknowledgements: *PN Review* and *Persian Miniatures* (Smith/Doorstop).

KEITH BLANDIN

Rubaiyat
(for Telajune)

Beyond the view of crossroads ringed with breath
her bed appears, the old-rose covers death
has smoothed and stilled; her fingers lie inert,
her nail-file lies beside her in its sheath.

The morning's work over, her final chore
was 'breaking up the sugar' just before
siesta, sitting cross-legged on the carpet,
her slippers lying neatly by the door.

The image of her room behind the pane,
though lost as the winding road shifts its plane,
returns on every straight, like signatures
we trace on glass, forget and find again.

I have inherited her tools: her anvil,
her axe, her old scrolled mat, but not her skill;
and who would choose to chip at sugar-blocks
when sugar-cubes are boxed beside the till?

The scent of lilacs from the road reminds me
of my own garden: a neighbouring tree
grows near the fence. At night its clusters loom
like lantern-moons, pearly-white, unearthly.

I don't mind that the lilac's roots aren't mine.
Its boughs are, and its blooms. It curves its spine
towards my soil and litters it with dying
stars: deadheads I gather up like jasmine.

My grandmother would rise and take my arm,
then sifting through the petals in her palm
would place in mine the whitest of them all:
'Salaam, dokhtaré-mahé-man, salaam!'

'Salaam, my daughter-lovely-as-the-moon!'
Would that the world could see me, Telajune,
through your eyes! Or that I could see a world
that takes such care to tend what fades so soon.

The Poulterer

His card shows nothing sinister. He stands
against a background sky, a farmyard scene:
against the duck-egg blue and fawn, his hands
are pale as vellum, sleeved in acorn-green.
His name, though scrolled in black like other names
from higher decks – The Hanged Man, Hierophant,
rich in papal gold, The Tower in flames –
his name, though less arcane, is more extant.
He deals in lower echelons than they:
in women, mad in chains, who hoot like owls;
in men who line the fence like ghosts in grey;
in little girls who dream of ginger cowls:
    of claws that pierce the railings of their beds
    where father stands; who dream in coxcomb reds.

The Bowl

Having reached the southern extremity of the marsh, the path begins to climb
the hills that confine the lake-basin. The ascent is steep and joyless; but it is
as nothing compared with the descent on the other side, which is long, precipit-
ous, and inconceivably nasty. This is the famous Kotal-i-Pir-i-Zan, or Pass of
the Old Woman.

Some writers have wondered at the origin of the name. I feel no such surprise.
On the contrary, I admire the apposite felicity of the title. For, in Persia, if one
aspired, by the aid of a local metaphor, to express anything that was peculiarly
uninviting, timeworn, and repulsive, a Persian old woman would be the first
and most forcible simile to suggest itself. I saw many hundreds of old women
during my travels in that country…and I crossed the Kotal-i-Pir-i-Zan, and I
can honestly say that whatever derogatory or insulting remarks the most copious
of vocabularies might be capable of expending upon the one, could be transfer-
red, with equal justice, to the other.

…At the end of the valley the track…makes a slight ascent, and then, at the
crest of the ridge,…discloses a steep and hideous descent, known to fame, or
infamy, as the Kotal-i-Dokhter, or Pass of the Maiden.

I do not know if the *dokhter* in question (the same word as the English daughter)
is supposed to have been allied by the filial tie to the Old Woman…but from
the strong family likeness between the pair, I feel justified in assuming the
relationship. As I descended the Daughter, and alternately compared and con-
trasted her features with those of the Old Woman, I fear that I irreverently
paraphrased a well-known line,

O matre laeda filia laedior!

GEORGE NATHANIEL CURZON, *Persia and the Persian Question*

NOTES
Chenar: Plane tree.
Lahaf-Doozee: The Quilt Sewer, who rejuvenates the down in old quilts.
Sineh Sefid: Mt White Breast.
Mer: Egyptian goddess of mother-love and waters.

I

The bowl is big and blue. A flash of leaf
along its rim is green, spring-green, lime
and herringbone. Across the glaze where fish swim,
across the loose-knit waves in hopscotch-black,
borders of fish-eye and cross-stitch, chestnut trees
throw shadows: candles, catafalques and barques
and lord knows what, what ghost of ancient seacraft,
what river-going name we give to shadows.

Inside the bowl, in clay and earth and limestone,
beneath the dust and loam, leaf forms lie
fossilised. They have come from mountain passes,
from orchards where no water runs or fields
with only threadbare shade for mares and mule foals.
They are named: cuneiform and ensiform,
spathulate and sagittate and their margins
are serrated, lapidary, lobed.

My book of botany is green: the gloss
of coachpaint, carriages, Babushka dolls,
the clouded genie jars of long ago.
Inside my bowl a womb of air revolves.
What tadpole of the stream, what holly-spine
of seahorse could be nosing at its shallows,
what honeycomb of sunlight, marbled-green
of malachite be cobbled in its hoop?

I squat, I stoop. My knees are either side
of bowl. My hands are eyes around its crescent.
The surface of its story feathers me.
My ears are all a-rumour. On a skyline
I cannot see a silhouette carves vase-shapes
into sky: baby, belly, breast, thigh;
an aeroplane I cannot hear has shark fins
and three black camels sleep in a blue, blue desert.

II

My bowl has cauled my memories. My bowl
has buried me. Hoofprints where Ali's horse
baulked at the glint of cutlasses have thrummed
against my eyelids. Caves where tribal women
stooped to place tin sconces, their tapers lit,
have scaffolded my skin. Limpet-pools
have scooped my gums, raising weals and the blue
of morning-glory furled around my limbs.

My bowl has smashed my boundaries: harebell
and hawthorn mingling in my thickened waist
of jasmine; catkin and *chenar*, dwarf-oak
and hazel hanging over torrents, deltas,
my seasons' arteries...*Lahaf-Doozee!*...
My retina is scarred with shadow-dances
and echoes run like hessian blinds across
my sleep; my ears are niches, prayer-rug arches.

Lahaf-Doozee! My backbone is an alley,
a pin-thin alley, cobblestoned
with hawkers' cries, a saddlebag of ribs.
The Quilt Man comes. He squats, he stoops, he spreads
his flattened bale, unslings his bow of heartwood
and plucks the string: *dang dang tok tok* and cotton
rising, rising, is snared around his thread,
snaking, swells in a cobra-head of fleece.

My ancestors have plumped their quilts with homespun,
in running-stitch have saved a legend's lining:
an infant in its hammock, safe in cloud,
who swung between the poles of quake and wall,
hung swaying to and fro: small and holy.
Lizards have kept their watch on lamplight: citrus-
peel in my mother's hand becoming baskets.
My bowl beneath the tap is scoured with leaves.

III

The white rooms of the house we glimpsed through pine,
quince and pomegranate are derelict.
Calendars of saint-days still cling to plaster,
drawing-pinned. Velvet-weavers, hammam-keepers
have rolled their weekdays in the rags, the closing
craft-bag of centuries. And worker bees
on hillsides, hiding in ceramic jars,
no longer yield the gold of robbers' honey.

High on a ledge, a white angora goat bleats...
I, too, will take my bowl and leave these wheatfields
speckled with hollyhocks, blue campanulas,
the threshing floors on roofs of sun-dried clay.
Over twigbridge, past camel-thorn and thistle
bristling with snake, through rock rib and ravine
I will lead my mule to the high ground, kneel
above the eyrie, spread my rug in shade.

Below me, as the sun goes down, marsh pools
will glimmer red. *Sineh Sefid* will be gashed
with gold, will change from rose to blue, from blue
to grey. My bowl will hold the bowl of sky
and as twilight falls I will stand and fling
its caul and watch it land as lake: a ring
where *rood* and *river* meet in peacock-blue
and peacock-green and a hundred rills cascade.

And evening's narrow pass will bring me down
to bowl, to sit at lakeside's old reflections:
those granite spurs no longer hard and cold
but furred in the slipstream of a lone oarsman.
And from its lap a scent will rise like *Mer*
from *mother-love* and *waters*; scent whose name
I owe to *Talat, gold* for grandmother:
Maryam, tuberose, for bowl, for daughter.

Baba Mostafa

He circles slowly and the walls of the room,
this Maryland cocoon, swirl as though the years
were not years but faces and he, at eighty,
in his warm woolly robe, were the last slow waltz.

'Children,' he would say, '*truly* love me!
And I have always, always loved children.'
'It's true,' she'd say, coming through the arch.
'Sarajune, you love Baba Mostafa, don't you?
D'you love Baba Mostafa or Maman Gitty, hah?
Here, eat this.' 'For God's sake, woman,
do you want her to choke! Come, Sarajune, dance…
da-dum, da-dum, da-dum, da-da…'

He circles slowly, the child on his shoulder
nestled like a violin and the ruches of a smile
on the corners of his lips as though the babygro'
beneath his hand were glissades of satin.

'Wunderschön! Das ist wunderschön!' He lingers
on the umlaut he learned as a student on a scholarship
from Reza Shah and on the lips of a Fraulein
whose embouchure lives on in him, takes him back
through all those years, through marriages, children,
reversals of fortune, remembering how in wartime
foodstuffs left his home for hers – manna from Isfahan,
sweetmeats from Yazd, dried fruit from Azarbaijan.

He circles slowly, on paisley whorls
that once were cypress trees bowing to the wind,
as though these 'perfect moslems' were reflections
of his coat-tails lifting on a breeze from the floor.

'I swear to God,' he blubbered, only days before
his laryngotomy, 'I was a good man. I never stole.
And if – and who can say? – you never had the father
my other children had, God knows it wasn't in my hands.'
'How is he?' they whispered in doorways as I buried
my butt-ends in beds of azaleas. Months later,

he writes: 'I can't eat *gut* and sleep *gut*.' He never could:
holding up *Der Spiegel*, in the small hours, to the lamp.

And now he circles, from room to room,
with a grandchild for company who step by step
outstrips him as he learns – relearns – to talk...
da-dum, da-dum, da-dum, da-da...

Haiku
A war-time picnic

On the verandah
the wet-nurse thinks of her own
pomegranate tree.

The river paddles
as we barbecue; Hassan
removes his serge-green.

I climb the noon-day
peak: a broken flip-flop thong
flutters at my feet.

Linda Saunders

LINDA SAUNDERS was born in Caterham, Surrey. She went to art school in Reigate, and then to Durham University where she read English. Sixteen years in Durham, interrupted by two in London and two in California near the Mojave desert (where her first son, the 'Freethinker', was born), gave her an affinity for the North East, now dissipated by living in Bath.

Apart from poetry, she is the author of numerous articles on art and artists, and in 1988 was shortlisted for the BP Arts Journalist of the Year. She has been poetry editor of *The Green Book*, and is now assistant editor of *Modern Painters*, the fine arts journal. ●

Acknowledgements: *Anglo-Welsh Review, The Green Book Anthology, The Rialto* and *South West Review*

A Freethinker's Baptism

You asked me to your baptism, over
your shoulder, on the way out of a door.
Sixteen years ago you were reluctant even
to be born, whimpered at cold blades of air.

Naked on steel scales you sprayed the doctor's
white coat with a five foot arc of water:
your unredeemed self, assertive,
recalcitrant, someone I began to love.

Now I'm an observer at a rite
in which I have no part: you made secret
preparations, washing your own white shirt.

Such a sceptic under my care, you mock
doubt itself, or was the sky too bare?
Out of the open you choose to enter

these distempered walls, a narrow aisle,
a font large as a family plot sunk
in lino tiles. Already the baptist

waist deep in the floor, lifts a dripping sleeve.
Intent you take his hand – guiding you down,
folding you back into your element:

another parting. You are under for seconds;
I hold my breath, but you come up laughing
with a rush of water, tossing back wet hair.

An impassioned sermon of blood and sins,
those swaying hymns, stiffened my resistance.
But now your flaring glance, beyond reason

moves me like a birth. Your shirt welds
in folds to your brown skin, you stand in pools.
And I stay dry, swept by your moment
of freedom, but not feeling free to cry.

The Lepidopterist's Dream
(after Arthur Rackham)

He sleeps fast-pinned to his dream
of a boy on a June meadow:
a flitting run then breath-held stalking
wary of his own shadow,
waiting for the wings to hammer
their pulse of colour on a cornflower eye.
He never dreamt of murder then
but a blink of scarlet on the body's hinge.

Fingers flutter to his throat
for now it changes: showcases
crack their glass like pupal skin,
the air is shivered crystal
and shadows glitter with a rain of pins.
A storm of butterflies and moths
beats upwards, lifting the dreamer's hair
on brilliant fans. Live things
smudge their dust on his lips
and blur the moon's edge with their wings.

Silences

Voices he describes in his air letters – the velvet lilt
and throaty wood-wind Suto, the looping whistles of birds –
she does not hear. Silence all the way from Africa thickens
her walls. Only the paper rustles, brittle grass on dry hide.
Her gaze drifts always from the page as if following
through dim viscous water the slow rise of bubbles which signal
her life where it's fixed, his anchor.

He will find his postcards propped in rows in the kitchen
to prove he was gone, remote: 'A view of Table Mountain
with its famous table cloth.' Lava of cloud spills
towards the sun-studded mosaic of Cape Town, a turquoise bay.
She flexes toes on the vinolay, chin between knees,
licking for comfort her own salt off her own skin,
not seeing what he sees. No more do the homesick whites

who complain of the lack of green and unreflecting rock
in an arid landscape. But you should walk into it,
he tells them, and her: see how the light lays a purple sheen
on skin, and children at the edge of a reed-coned village
clap and cup their hands for an apple, making you bounteous,
and the proteas, even in winter, open their crowns of red
soft brushes round cymes of packed feather.

His breath moistens her neck and hair in an English heatwave –
even yet she would not believe him here, if that silence
had not withdrawn. Now they make their own, where travellers' tales
leave a fading bow of cloud long after the tiny silver plane
has passed, its rumble gone. She need not see or hear, but reads
without wandering, while knowing the proteas, unpacked
from his suitcase for her room, sip water and begin to breathe.

Her Bed

His weight in the bed was
her body's constant direction.
Naked on summer nights
she swayed in the warm hammock
of his breath.

Now the sheet is stretched across
the place that keeps his impression.
Mostly she sleeps on her own
side, yet in the heat searches
that cool zone.

Practice Board

Rust spots his knives now: I never
touch them. Or cry. But test
my figure in its sequined one-piece,
rehearse our triumphs, breast
ghostly applause.

My thighs, even my hips, still fit
the outline, though he had to thicken
black paint at my waist of recent years.
I'll slice that off you, he'd wink,
if I fancied a cake.

Such grace! He was like a dancer,
fluid, spinning. So tender, rocking his knives.
A tree swaying, then steady as prayer
in the bated breeze – my life
his balance.

Just the breath of the blade, sharp intake
before the thud, shiver of the board
down my skin. Keener and keener
he draws me – If I died
how they'd love me!

His last throw sticks red ribbon, undoes
the bow at the side of my throat,
leaving it like a blood trickle as
his hand ushers me out.
Again, again.

Briar Wood

BRIAR WOOD was born in 1958 in Taumarunui, a small town in New Zealand, of Kiwi, Scottish, English, as well as distant Maori and Portuguese descent. She has always felt torn between her roots in the rural King Country and the Waikato, where she spent her earliest years (and later taught in a school), and the city of Auckland, where she went to school and university, did an MA in English and trained as a teacher.

She came to Britain in 1983 to study feminist literary theory, and has mainly lived in London since then. ●

Fado

He always loved the sea
so much more than me
you could envisage a remoteness
in his mao mao eyes.

Nipples like radiate limpets
and sandpaper hand shake.
Born under the sign of Pisces,
he was perpetually drawn

towards large bodies of water.
Bold as the break
on a West Coast beach.
Swept off cold feet

swimming in neritic zones.
Anemone tentacle kisses,
clung like a succubus.
Chiton armour tight.

Nobody found out
the discarded garments
or how he drowned.
I only know when

I open my mouth
bubbles stutter out.

Aria

Regnava nel silenzio
alta la notte e bruna

maraschino

trickle and slick
Blackpool rules
tacky as molasses

torchlight toils
morepork morepork
and mamba coils

coloratura

tui

above Southern Alps
calm as Mantovani
Lippizanner dressage

in a haven of valium
spate
a stilus scraped
across the latent

Lake Lausanne

ice thin windows

chalk on blackboard
static cackles

crude oil feuds
internal combustion flutters
polythene crackles

hopeless motives

reprise

how sound barriers

varoom

black box from Lockerbie

tessitura illusions
deep as the lift shaft
at Covent Garden

stalls

each Milford Peak

all Bridal Veil Falls

Pale et blonde dort sous l'eau profonde

Mare Serenitatis

gratis

Me tradi

but alas we are neither
Lizzie Siddal in the bath

Ophelia or

Kiri Te Kanawa

going to Rarohanga
Hine nui te Po

Mutter!
Der Holle Rache kocht in meinem Herzen

Moulding Heathcliff

Faithless, a bit screwed up,
to begin with, jab him –
a wishbone in the ribcage.
Let him bastardise
the accents of childhood.

Crush his sense of humour
until he can't laugh
in public, at our desire
for success. Shove him
under a microphone. Insist

that he breathe poetry
into the banal exotica
of commonplace dreams.
Above all, let him be
an ordinary man.

The Bridal Feet

Goose girl ganders
on the way from market –
strut and kerfuffle.

A dead giveaway.
Pointing forward –
leaden arrowheads.

no dainty tiptoes –
more like sliced bread.
Doorstoppers.

Sinking fangs
in the morning lawn.
They are strainer posts.

A precise white
leather of new shoes
worn neither in nor out.

Stowaways –
in some corner
of a bottom drawer.

Squeaking
albino mice.
Pint sized.

They peek
full of gossip
from the lace curtain

a modest frock.
Garterless –
the flash of ankle

Marriage is like
trying to climb Mt Everest
in stilettos

said a wedding guest
with black accessories
her skirt a rubric red.

Falling Apart

Did you read about
the husband and wife
skydiving team?

She collided
on the way down
with a student
and got knocked
unconscious.

He made a few
rapid calculations
and plunged

without opening the chute,
rolling himself
into the smallest
human cannonball

it is possible to imagine
glissando and Tibetan poppies.

He managed to catch her
before they hit the ground

somewhat off target.
She had two broken legs;
he was unharmed.

This report never said
what happened to the pupil.

Quite Like a Prayer

Sunday in St Charles Square.
A rare minute's silence
before rugged sun up.
Vi, the landlady, aimless,
stunned among geranium strains
in the garish garden.
What Gethsemane. Her only son,
a truck driver, died yesterday
abruptly. Heart attack.

Upstairs, k.d. lang and *Shadowlands*.
Along the street, where religiously,
Saturday acid house parties take precedence
Neneh Cherry, *Raw Like Sushi*, spins.

Mandatory belly button on the cover.
I try Madonna next, laconic,
crass, in the aftermath of Plath
that Marilyn Monroe of poetry.
Washed-out jeans, and amethyst
gules of rosary. Chiffon-topped,
the scented sleeve releases
cinnamon and patchouli –
overlaid by wafts of bacon.
A dedication to her mother.

The lodger from Galway,
whose wife committed suicide,
pissed again last night, as most nights,
opens a can of Guinness. Sssssss
stretches on the deck chair.
The hottest summer in living memory.
Yesterday, his back basted
to the subcutaneous. He couldn't sleep.
Rings the doorbell, persistently
at eight. I administer calamine
and witch-hazel with somnambulent hands.

By this time, the multiple inhabitants
of the top floor flat
might have been comatose
an hour or two. A couple had
a barney on the porch last night.
'No you can't stay in my room.
You jerk, get off!'

Another vagrant drunk broke the banister
whooping 'Ruapehu!'
smashed the rock crystal vase
full of plastic daffodils
in a dog-shit cluttered gutter.

The tasteful 18th century prints
nicked by an itinerant epicure
have been replaced with calendar close-up
cutouts. Owl eyes. Falcon beak.
One bike has a puncture. Mine?
with kryptonite padlock missing.

Next-door, James chips at sandstone
sculpture, the one backyard implant
except a rampant grape vine.
And Cathy, miniscule bikinied, reading
Lives of the Great Philosophers.

Dingle waves, oleaginous armed –
his Motoguzzi an unsolved jigsaw
and comes over for a smoke.

The telephone goes. Hopefully
it's Marino or Sophie.

Adèle Geras

ADÈLE GERAS was born in 1944 in Jerusalem and spent her early childhood in many countries, including North Borneo and the Gambia. She studied Modern Languages at St Hilda's College Oxford, and was a singer and teacher of French before becoming a full-time writer in 1976. Her many books for children and young adults include *Voyage*, *Apricots at Midnight* and *The Tower Room*.

She has had poems published in several magazines and in Littlewood's *Northern Poetry One*. In 1987 she won (with Pauline Stainer) the Poetry Business Competition with her pamphlet collection *Up on the Roof* (Smith/Doorstop). She is married with two daughters and lives in Manchester. ●

Acknowledgements: *Northern Poetry One* (Littlewood Press, 1989).

Needleworks

> *The yere of Our Lord being 1657*
> *if ever I have any thoughts about the time*
> *when I went to Oxford, as it may be I may,*
> *when I have forgotten the time,*
> *to satisfi my self, I may look in this paper*
> *and find it.*
> *I went to Oxford in the yere of 1644...*

The King and his court are here.
My cousin Beth lives
in a house beside the walls.
My mother left me.
Father says
she looks on me from Heaven.

I keep her box of silks,
pages of printed patterns
like a book.

Here is Winter,
an old man in a bonnet
rocking in a chair.
At his feet, a brazier,
at his back, a river

waiting for the colour of ice.
I shall sew red
into the fire
and flames like a fountain
will edge his robes with saffron.

Winter has a cat.
It sits and watches him,
watches empty trees,
tall houses, a bellows
waiting for embers
and logs bound into bundles.

Satin	satin stitch
embroidery silk	stem stitch
metal threads	laid work
seed pearls	padding
spangles	petit point

The lions' heads
are threaded with bronze.
Birds fly in the border,
pearls in white wings.

Lady Autumn's
among her golden sheaves.
Behind her,
blue silk
and green silk
of the river.
Trees branch to feathers,
clouds like veils
touch a pink castle.
Always evening light
for Lady Autumn.

> *and my being there 2 yeres,*
> *for I went in 1644*
> *and I stayed there 1645*
> *and cam away in 1646,*
> *and I was almost 12 yeres of age when I went*
> *and made an end of my cabinette at Oxford…*

Stitches
tell stories:

Joseph and his brothers
at the well,
Deborah and Barak,
and Jael and Sisera.
The tent flutters,
open. *He asked*
for water and she gave him milk
and butter in a lordly dish
then killed him.

Cousin Beth
is caring for a soldier
wounded in battle.
I help her.
I keep the watches
beside his bed
and mark his fevered breathing.

Sometimes I think:
his life is my silk,
tied to my needle.
Stitches gather.
I make pictures
to fill the hours
till my life shall start:
when the war ends,
when the soldier wakes,
when he looks on me.

> *and my cabinette was mad up in the yere of 1656*
> *at London.*

The soldier left our house.
I embroidered long weeks:
every thread a vein
every pearl a tear
every stitch a sorrow
every needle a small dagger
drawing blood.

My cabinet holds trinkets:
letters, chains,
locks of hair, and flowers
pressed to memories.

I have ritten this to satisfi my self
and those that shall inquir about it.

    Hannah Smith.

Sampler 1850

If I look up
from the window seat, I see the garden.
The flowers are ragged after rain.
Soon, autumn will be here.
Already, leaves have fallen on the path.

I turn to my sampler.
The flowers are in lines
evenly spaced, and when I've finished them
I'll write my name, and numbers
and the date.
When winter comes, I will have started
my picture of a house.

Where shall I go
when I reach the edge of the canvas?

Wall-hanging 1920

A story told and told:

My great-grandmother, always called The Bobbeh,
demonstrates devotion,
attention to detail
and a sense of smell that was the envy of Jerusalem.

She was blind in old age.
Her daughter held and twisted
the domestic threads.

At night-time, beds like water-lilies
opened in the dining-room.
Tight-folded sheets unfurled in corridors.
Unerringly, The Bobbeh
crossed yellow tiles and reached the linen chest.

There she would sniff each pillow and pronounce
every child's name in turn, with no mistakes.

'This one is Sara's' (recognising smells)
'Reuben's and Dina's'...on and on
a murmuring variation on ten notes.

Outside the story:
the white filigree of crochet,
the squares and diamonds of drawn-threadwork
bordering each pillow-slip
on every perfectly distributed pillow
have stiffened now, smell of green soap
and the grey weight of the iron,
pressing flat. The work of her young hands.

Her seeing shrank. Her needle swelled
thick as a chicken bone.
It plunged through canvas dragging blanket wool,
made crosses in child's colours:
the peaks and dips of hastily-drawn hills.

The Bobbeh's cross-stitch mountains
covered a whole wall
in the end.
Uneven green and red, orange and black,
purple, white and yellow chevrons
rose from the horizon of her couch
almost to the ceiling.

Tapestry 1971

She had intended it for me
because she had no children of her own.
'Take it with you,' she said
'I don't need it.' If I die (she meant)
someone else will have the trouble
of packing, of despatching.
And what if it were lost?
Or the glass could break,
some unforeseen sharp thing
tear the canvas...oh,
the whole tapestry could reach you
shredded.

She prepares for dreamed cataclysms.
Now, I'm here.
Tomorrow, I'm going home,
so let me take it.

They check it at the airport.
Are there terrorists
who parcel bombs
like pictures, framed?
Arrange explosives flat
behind the glass?
The men on duty
unwrap it, wrap it up again
unlovingly.
Patterns elude them,
colours slide past their eyes,
It is not what they feared.

It hangs in an alcove.
The jade tree on the TV set
almost reaches it.

'Petit point,' she said,
giving it to me.
The stitches are smaller than sesame seeds:
huddled apostrophes, slanting to the right.
The canvas was starched gauze –
a fine white mesh.
'I don't like printed patterns…being told
where to go and in what shade of pink.
I follow from one colour to the next.
When one thread ends
another calls to me.
I never know, never knew
the path the silk would take,
how it would come out.
Mother said I'd tire of it.
She died too soon to see it on the wall.
Towards the end,
criss-crossing lines appeared
in black: a colour
I'd been trying to avoid.'

I think:
there was a plan known
by the fingers. The little glitter
of a needle's eye
foresaw circles
triangles
dots
moons
balconies
stars
curves
rectangles
upended squares
sloping to rows of geometric hills.

Look: this yellow disc
could be a lamp
or an apricot
or the sun.

Embroidered Picture 1987

You and I see houses
in a suburban street:
privet hedges, nineteen-thirties windows,
trees taken for granted,
Sunday-painted gates,
blue thrown over everything
like a scarf: unremarked.

She saw
curves, lines, perspectives,
twenty possibilities of green,
pink roofs shrinking to distance,
threads massing into branches.
She framed everything with lace –
a thin cloud border for the pale washed sky.

Jackie Kay

Acknowledgements: *Beautiful Barbarians* (Onlywomen), *Black Women Talk Poetry*, *Crisis and Creativity* (Rodopi), *New Voices* (Radio 3) and *Pi Ti Commonwealth Poetry Journal*.

JACKIE KAY was born in 1961 in Edinburgh, and grew up in Glasgow. Her first play *Chiaroscuro* was presented by Theatre of Black Women in 1986 and is published in *Lesbian Plays* (Methuen); her second, *Twice Over*, was staged by Gay Sweatshop in 1988 and published in *Gay Sweatshop: Four Plays and a Company* (Methuen). Her poems have appeared in various anthologies, including *Angels of Fire* (Chatto) and *The New British Poetry* (Paladin); her first collection, *The Adoption Papers*, is due from Bloodaxe in 1991, and a dramatised version of the book is being broadcast in BBC Radio 3's *Drama Now* series in 1990. She lives in London with her son, and is currently Hammersmith and Fulham's writer in residence. ●

The Visit

I thought I'd hid everything
that there wasnie wan
give away sign Left

I put Marx Engels Lenin (no Trotsky)
in the airing cupboard – she'll no be
checking out the towels surely

All the copies of the *Daily Worker*
I shoved under the sofa
the dove of peace I took down from the loo

A poster of Paul Robeson
saying give him his passport
I took down from the kitchen

I left a bust of Burns
my detective stories
and the *Complete Works of Shelley*

She comes at 11.30 exactly.
I pour her coffee
from my new Hungarian set

And foolishly prays she willnae
ask its origins – honestly
this baby is going to my head

She crosses her legs on the sofa
I fancy I hear the *Daily Workers*
rustle underneath her

Well she says, you have an interesting home
She sees my eyebrows rise
It's different she qualifies

Hell and I've spent all morning
trying to look ordinary
– a lovely home for the baby

She buttons her coat all smiles
I'm thinking
I'm on the home run

But just as we get to the last post
her eye catches at the same times as mine
a red ribbon with twenty world peace badges

Clear as a hammer and sickle
on the wall
oh she says are you against nuclear weapons?

To Hell with this. Baby or no baby.
Yes   I says. Yes yes yes.
I'd like this baby to live in a nuclear free environment

Oh. Her eyes light up.
I'm all for peace myself she says
and sits down for another cup of coffee.

The Telling Part

Ma mammy bot me oot a shop
Ma mammy says I was a luvly baby

Ma mammy picked me (I wiz the best)
your mammy had to take you (she'd no choice)

Ma mammy says she's no really ma mammy
(just kid on)

It's a bit like a part you've rehearsed so well
you can't play it on the opening night
She says my real mammy is away far away
Mammy why aren't you and me the same colour
    But I love my mammy whether she's real or no
My heart started rat tat tat like a tin drum
all the words took off to another planet
Why

But I love ma mammy whether she's real or no

I could hear the upset in her voice
I says *I'm not your real mother*
though Christ knows why I said that
If I'm not who is, but all my planned speech
went out the window

    She took me when I'd nowhere to go
    my mammy is the best mammy in the world OK

After mammy telt me she wisnae my real mammy
I was scared to death she was gonnie melt
or something or mibbe disappear in the dead
of night and somebody would say she wis a fairy
godmother. So the next morning I felt her skin
to check it was flesh, but mibbe it was just
a good imitation. How could I tell if my mammy
was a dummy with a voice spoken by someone else
So I searches the whole house for clues
but I never found nothing. Anyhow a day after
I got my guinea pig and forgot all about it.

I always believed in the telling anyhow.
You can't keep something like that secret
I wanted her to think of her other mother
out there thinking that child I had will be
seven today eight today all the way up to
god knows when. I told my daughter –
I bet your mother's never missed your birthday
How could she?

Bette Davis

Maybe it's really Bette Davis I want
to be the good twin or even better the bad
one or a nanny who drowns a baby in a bath
I'm not sure maybe I'd prefer Katharine
Hepburn tossing my red hair, having a hot
temper. I says to my teacher *Can't I be
Elizabeth Taylor*, drunk and fat and she
just laughed, not much chance of that.
I went for an audition for *The Prime
of Miss Jean Brodie*. I didn't get a part
even though I've been acting longer
that Beverley Innes. So I have. Honest.

Angela Davis

On my bedroom wall is a big poster
of Angela Davis who is in prison
right now for nothing at all
except she wouldn't put up with stuff.

My mum says she is *only* 26
which seems really old to me
but my mum says it is young
just imagine, she says, being on
America's Ten Most Wanted People's List at 26!
I can't.
Angela Davis is the only female person
I've seen (except for a nurse on TV)
who looks like me. She has big hair like mine
that grows out instead of down.
My mum says it's called an *Afro*.
If I could be as brave as her when I get older
I'll be OK.
Last night I kissed her goodnight again
and wondered if she could feel the kisses
in prison all the way from Scotland.
Her skin is the same too you know.
I can see my skin is that colour
but most of the time I forget
so sometimes when I look in the mirror
I give myself a bit of a shock
and say to myself *Do you really look like this?*
as if I'm somebody else. I wonder if she does that.
I don't believe she killed anybody.
It is all a load of phoney lies.
My dad says it's a set up.
I asked him if she'll get the electric chair
like them Roseberries he was telling me about.
No he says the world is on her side.
Well how come she's in there then I thinks
I worry she's going to get the chair.
I worry she's worrying about the chair.
My dad says she'll be putting on a brave face.
He brought me a badge home which I wore
to school. It says FREE ANGELA DAVIS
And all my pals says 'Who's she?'

From Generations

The sun went out just like that
almost as if it had never been
hard to imagine now the way it fell
on treetops, thatched roofs, people's faces.
Suddenly the trees lost their nerves
and the grass passed the wind on
blade to blade, fast as gossip.

Years later, the voices still come close
especially in dreams, not distant echoes
loud – a pneumatic drill – deeper and deeper still.
I lived the scandal, wore it casual
as a summer's dress, Jesus sandals
all but the softest whisper:
she's lost an awful lot of weight.

Now my secret is the hush of heavy curtains drawn.
I dread strange handwriting
sometimes jump when the phone rings
she is all of nineteen and legally able
At night I lie practising my lines
but 'sorry' never seems large enough
nor 'I can't see you, yes, I'll send a photograph.'

I was pulled out with forceps
left a gash down my left cheek
four months inside a glass cot
but
she came faithful from Glasgow to Edinburgh
and peered through the glass
she would not pick another baby.

I don't know what diseases
come down my line
when dentist and doctors ask
the old blood questions about family runnings
I tell them: I have no nose or mouth or eyes
to match, no spitting image or dead cert
my face watches itself in the glass

I have my parents who are not of the same tree
and you keep trying to make it matter
the blood, the tie, the passing down
generations.
We all have our contradictions
the ones with the mother's nose and father's eyes
have them
the blood does not bind confusion
yet I confess to my contradiction
I want to know my blood.

I know my blood.
It is dark ruby red and comes
regular and I use Lillets
I know my blood when I cut my finger
I know what my blood looks like.

It is the well, the womb, the fucking seed.
Here, I am far away to wonder
what were their faces like
who were my grandmothers
what were the days like
passed in Scotland
the land I come from
the soil in my blood.

Put it this way:
I know she thinks of me often
when the light shows its face
or the dark skulks behind hills
she conjures me up or I just appear
when I take the notion, my slippers
are silent and I walk through doors.

She's lying in bed; I wake her up
a pinch on her cheek is enough
then I make her think of me for hours
the best thing I can steal is sleep
I get right under the duvet and murmur
you'll never really know your mother
I know who she thinks I am – she's made a blunder.

S.J. Litherland

MOIRA CONWAY

S.J. LITHERLAND is a freelance writer and tutor. She lives in Durham, where she brought up a daughter and a son, and has recently finished studying English at University College London. She is currently co-editing *The Poetry of Perestroika* with Peter Mortimer for Iron Press. In 1988 she collaborated with her daughter, artist Rachel Levitas, to produce a book of etchings and poems, *Half Light*, launched at the Rebecca Hossack Gallery, London.

Her collection *The Long Interval* was published by Bloodaxe in 1986 as a pamphlet and in the *Fourpack #1* anthology ●

Acknowledgements: *Iron* and *Oxford Magazine*; *The Long Interval* and *Half Light*.

The Long Interval

The sea black and grey
in the spring night.
We watch the unformed
wave run feverishly.

Suddenly in the darkness
a mouth of light opens
and swallows itself
not wide enough to call.

We hear the faint smack
of its lips as the sound
is eclipsed by the dark
waters' rise and fall.

The sea black and grey
in the spring night.
In the darkness we wait
for a new mouth to alight

somewhere on the water
before drowning itself.
The vanished voice is heard
in the long interval.

The Wake

From the moment we heard their music
on the evening steel water, water
slipping past our moored boat, draining
light from the deadening sky, we waited
for the singers. They struck onto the scene
as four arrows on the slow open curve
of the river. Four long narrow punts
were moving precisely parallel,
in harmony with their singers dressed
for an Edwardian boating party.

The four steering puntsmen, without
a splash on their suits, lifted
their poles in unison, four poles aloft,
striking the water together as they sang,
trailing through the confused screw
of their wake, their single
purpose. The formation swept by,
piloted only inches apart, phantoms
without human error. Was it our wake?
We could still hear their singing.

A Synagogue in Samarkand

A small worn street with side gulleys
of running water, the colour of pearl
and taint of drains. We are looking
for a synagogue behind the market
in Samarkand. Children cling to us.
It is hot. One of them is holding
a live hen upside down, dangling it
like a shopping basket. They all point
to a door in the wall which we pass.

It is intricately carved in Islamic
style and locked.
                          A boy circling
on a bicycle says: *My Uncle is the Rabbi!*
I'll fetch him.

                          I stare into brown eyes,
almond Jewish eyes which have looked out
of so many photographs, out of a past
I thought lost.

The children chant: *The Rabbi comes!*
The Rabbi comes! But it is an old woman,
the opener of the door to our party
three thousand miles from home.

Are you Jews?
I venture: My children are half-Jewish –
She smiles. The door is unlocked.

There is a small yard and I fear
the poverty of the ghetto. Among
us there is an anti-semite, a Russian
guide who has declared himself:
I don't like Jews. Do you like Jews?

An inner double door, another
in filigree work. The woman motions:
The Synagogue. I am the cleaner.

                          We enter
into sudden space. Startling white walls
with plasterwork like lace, dazzling
as a wedding cake. Blue domed ceiling.
Panelling of finely carved wood, fretted
like the doors. A central dais is draped
in velvet, surrounded by plain benches
as if drawn around for conversation.

The Rabbi arrives
in clean ironed shirt and trousers;
he looks enquiring, summoned to his synagogue.

He is pleased at our questions,
There are a hundred Jews in my community.
We have been here three hundred years
and came from Bukhara where we have lived
a thousand years since travelling from Iran.

We speak Hebrew.
He used the word *Yvrit*, not the Russian.

I am hoping to visit Israel next year.
Some of us have already gone.

                              Would he stay?
No, Samarkand is my home.

He opens a carved cupboard and draws out
a velvet box containing a scroll:
Our treasure. It was the Torah,
written down in beautiful script
by one of the community, a hundred
and twenty years ago. A rainbow
coloured chiffon marks a page.

We all shake hands.

Are you Christians?
The total is three atheists.
I offer: I am a Communist.
He smiles. Here it is a commonplace,

and I remember the women in the market
in the brightly coloured silk dresses
who had shouted: *Tell about our good life.*

[Samarkand, 1987]

Torah: first five books of the Bible.

The Debt Problem

I must tell my story. Listen.
There will be a number of things.
Without a pause, or a metaphor,

I will relate my day. Music
will play in the background.
I hear your dutiful listening.

It doesn't matter. Inside
there is a kind of cosiness
without heat. Outside, winter.

Money is impossible. My life
is frail, my economy *Polish*
and I need substantial aid

to buy freedom. Yes this
is my lack-lustre capitalism,
two rooms I do not own.

I fantasise that I can buy
good food. Clothes are my
Christmas presents.

So many people want to sell
things to me. My debts are making
love, new younger debts will arise.

[Newcastle, 1989]

Rachel Blake

Acknowledgements: *Country Life*, *New Poetry 4* (Arts Council) and *Tribune*.

RACHEL BLAKE was born in Dorking, spent her early childhood in rural Surrey, and then studied English at Durham University and art at the Slade School. She worked on the land and in advertising, and as a teacher in schools, in further education, in a small university in Lesotho, and with disturbed children. She now lives in the country in Surrey.

She co-wrote (with Pat Arrowsmith) *To Asia in Peace* (Sidgwick & Jackson, 1972), an account of non-violent peace action in Cambodia and Thailand. Her paintings and drawings have been exhibited, and her poems have appeared in many magazines and anthologies, and she has published reviews and articles in several newspapers. She was a 3rd prize winner in the Bloodaxe Books national poetry competition in 1987. ●

The Pale Boy and the Old Woman

The car dropped the pallid boy
Who lived in monotone.
He knocked at the green side door
Above scrubbed stone.

He ran to find the old woman
– To taste her grains –
The cold draughts puffed in the passage
Like wine in his veins.

Past the room with the marble angel
Where Miss Power sat
In velvet alongside her crutch
Behind frosty net.

Knew the room with the billiard table
– William pears ripening,
And O for the Wings of a Dove
On a Sunday evening.

On the netted flesh of her hands
Rivulets ran,
Potatoes dropped from the iron
Blade to the pan

– It stood on a kitchen table
Wavy with wear
The fire in the black stove
Red and clear.

From the tip of her nose a stray
Diamond rolled,
She said, 'You get more juicy
When you grow old.'

She opened the crumbling conservatory
With the six tomatoes,
She pressed the lemon verbena
Under his pale nose.

Her daughters steamed out of the wash-house
With a gust of noise,
The sheets rose in the copper
In tumescent haze.

The apple trees leaned to the thin brook
That edged the town,
It flowed with a thin town tinkle,
A weave of herring-bone.

The car returned him at twelve
To the grey-roofed
Mansion of monotones
Where nothing moved.

But the old woman incandesced,
Flamed inside him.
He knew it was a rehearsal.
He bode his time.

Transformations

I

The bricks of their quiet house were bright as rose
With sun that could not pierce the frozen zone
In which she circled back and forth from home
In brown, constricted, to a fixed refrain:

I cannot feel. I cannot feel. Charles is
A sensitive, loyal husband. We have one
Happily-married daughter, a lawyer son.

II

Her abstracted curator husband took the car
To the Museum; his hands were gentle on the wheel.

III

The girl he loved was carefully boxed, until
At last, and suddenly, he saw clearly through
His newly-brightened lenses, and the two
Slipped gratefully into a flat near Kennington
– The Hampstead house and car were left with Joan.

IV

She was a mollusc drifting with the tides,
Tentacles waving in a sad, warmer sea.
Abandoned, she smiled softly, her hair down,
At windy corners, Platform 1 at Camden Town.

V

Then flesh crept onto her bones, and mastery into her.
Her hair grew heavier, it swung. She drove
The Renault, intent behind dark horn frames.
The house was Under Offer. Came the day
Of Pickford's removal. She had gone away.

Childhood Lane

The oaks written across tongues of rose
Plumbed me, suddenly. That cold still
Energises, the sharp shreds of hedge,
And webbed ice, dry along the verges
– Later the lucid puddles of spring
Filled them. Now the hand in my head
Dips and catches the bend by the larch wood
– Cilial in April, with nutleaves.

On the right the breadline cottages,
Worked in, lapsing. All known and stored.
The lane is a layer I contain.
We had two feelings at the cross-roads:
There were ruled lines on corrugated barns
– And bigger skies struck with the colour of speedwells.

Lifeline

I feel the need
For a fishpond

And have the intention
To sink one, low,

Like a long-ago
Pool by a farm

Where the back-
to-the-wild carp hung

Red and black,
Possessors of wholeness

Coming slow
Above the moulding mud.

In deep water
Red blood is fed

– Even the globed kind's
Gold scales are tinged red

For danger. Bone-packed,
Fish resist drowning.

All leaps will freeze
In the act, impulse go

Without the unease
Of fish twisting below.

Gwyneth Lewis

GWYNETH LEWIS was born in 1959 in Cardiff. Her first language was Welsh, and she went to a bilingual comprehensive in Pontypridd. After reading English at Cambridge, she went to America as a Harkness Fellow, studying at Harvard and Columbia, and working in New York as a freelance journalist, and then did research at Oxford on literary forgeries. She is now working as a television journalist in Cardiff.

Acknowledgements: *Poetry Review* and *Verse*.

She was one of the writers featured in *Poetry Review*'s 'New British Poets' special issue in 1987, and won an Eric Gregory Award in 1988. She was the Welsh Language Editor of *Poetry Wales* for two years, and her first book of Welsh poems, *Sonedau Redsa*, was published by Gwasg Gomer in 1990. ●

From Welsh Espionage

V

Welsh was the mother tongue, English was his.
He taught her the body by fetishist quiz,
father and daughter on the bottom stair:
'Dy benelin yw *elbow*, dy wallt di yw *hair*,

chin yw dy ên di, *head* yw dy ben.'
She promptly forgot, made him do it again.
Then he folded her *dwrn* and, calling it *fist*,
held it to show her *knuckles* and *wrist*.

'Let's keep it from Mam, as a special surprise.
Lips yw gwefusau, llygaid yw *eyes*.'
Each part he touched in their secret game
thrilled as she whispered its English name.

The mother was livid when she was told.
'We agreed, no English till four years old!'
She listened upstairs, her head in a whirl.
Was it such a bad thing to be Daddy's girl?

IX *Advice on Adultery*

The first rule is to pacify the wives
if you're presented as the golden hope
at the office party. You're pure of heart,
but know the value of your youthful looks.
Someone comments on your lovely back.
Talk to the women, and avoid the men.

In work they treat you like one of the men
and soon you're bored with the talk of the wives
who confide in you about this husband's back,
or that husband's ulcer. They sincerely hope
you'll never have children – it ruins your looks.
And did you know David has a dicky heart?

You go to parties with a beating heart,
start an affair with one of the men.
The fact you've been taking care of your looks
doesn't escape the observant wives
who look at you sourly. Cross your fingers and hope
that no one's been talking behind your back.

You go to the Ladies. On your way back
one of them stops you for a heart to heart.
She hesitates, then expresses the hope
that you won't take offence, but men will be men,
and a young girl like you, with such striking looks...
She's heard nasty rumours from some of the wives.

She knows you're innocent, but the wives,
well, jump to conclusions from the way it looks...
In a rage, you resolve she won't get him back,
despite the pressure from the other wives.
They don't understand – you'll stick with the men,
only they are *au fait* with affairs of the heart.

You put it to him that you're living in hope.
He grants that you're beautiful, but looks
aren't everything. He's told the men,
who smirk and wink. So now you're back

to square one, but with a broken heart.
You make your peace with the patient wives.

Don't give up hope at the knowing looks.
Get your own back, have a change of heart:
Ignore the men, start sleeping with the wives.

X

From Craig y Foelallt I can see it all –
the church, the chapel, the dry stone bridge,
the road that leads to the vicarage,
Catherine's house by the village hall.

They're playing football. From the hoots and cries
I count up the score: Llanddewi two,
the visitors nil. Children I knew
have grown into farmers I don't recognise.

I watch the living, while overhead
two kites are working the valley floor,
looking for movement. Me they ignore
because I'm spying on the dead.

XI

So this is the man you dreamt I had betrayed.
I couldn't have saved him if I'd stayed.

He's old as his language. On his bony knees
his hands are buckled like wind-blown trees

that were straight in his youth. His eyes are dim,
brimming with water. If you talk to him

he'll mention people whom you never knew,
all in their graves. He hasn't a clue

who you are, or what it is you want
on your duty visits to Talybont.

This is how languages die – the tongue
forgetting what it knew by heart, the young

not understanding what, by rights, they should.
And vital intelligence is gone for good.

The Bad Shepherd

Cornelius Varro knows his husbandry
and he maintains a flourishing estate:
'My mutes stand guard at the entrance gate.
Vowels I lodge with my hired men,
half-vowels sit by the cattle pen.
Of course, I let the spirants work the field,
as they're teaching the clover how to yield
to consonantal chimings from the church.'
But I'm uncouth and keep lip service back.

For I'm the one who herds his fields of wheat,
speaks softly till the stalks are white,
the ripe ears heavy. Then I sow my spite
and laugh to see how the rows stampede,
as I spread sedition with the highland wind
till they're wrecked and broken. Then he sends men round
and I watch in silence as they slowly reap
his yearly tribute from my grudging ground.

The Building Site
(for David)

'Odds and sods,' cried the empty hod,
'give the rafters a wedding spree,
for the lone plank's married a parquet floor
and my bricks have deserted me.

The guttering's ready for rain on the run,
and the lintel's forgotten the plane,
the patio's swept, all furnished for fun,
the plaster-dust swilled down the drain.'

But the house sang back the mourning hod:
'All grouting is gravel and even the level
can't make a crock newel stay true.
Be brave, and I'll buckle the architrave
till the builders come looking for you.
I'll block up the drains, and trip-wire the mains,
and make sure that the roof joists grow,
for the damp is a wizard and the building's a hazard
and the sun is a tick-tack-toe,
oh, the sun is a tick-tack-toe.'

On Mayon Volcano

Two summers ago this hot spring turned cold
but the bathers still come with guitars and beer.
Lovingly, girls wash their long black hair,
knowing they're watched from the far shore's shade.
Maybe Mayon the beautiful is getting old.

The concrete mermaid's set a little apart.
A young boy clings to her crumbling lap,
touches a nipple, her hair, her lips
with wonder, then turns and duck-dives back.
There's luck to be had from her broken heart.

Of all the bathers, the mermaid alone
feels terrible pressure from the cone above.
The swimmers tread water and think of love.
But she knows that ash can be razor-sharp,
that no one can swim in rivers of stone.

The Cut of Women's Clothes
(in a costume museum)

These *tableaux vivants* take us through
the rise of the hem, the fall of the waist
and show what men and women do
when dressed in the very best of taste.

Unable to move her head to say
what she thinks of the wimp at the mantelpiece
she, as she must, has to turn away
and show us the back of her smart pelisse.

In a cuirass bodice, with its hooks and eyes,
she snubs a suitor, hair black as sin;
from his sofa he feels her stockinged thighs
burn in their cage of crinoline.

On the arm of her husband, the blushing bride
has risked a spectacular décolletage
but he knows already what wonders reside
in the skin-tight ivory silk corsage.

Three Queen Anne virgins dance and sing,
their lithe limbs draped in Grecian folds,
the muslin's kept wet to make it cling.
Two will be killed by a classical cold.

The French Revolution's the final scene:
the lady's prepared, wears a simple coat,
hair shorn, neck bared for the guillotine,
a coral necklace round her tingling throat.

Vuyelwa Carlin

PETER BARTLETT

VUYELWA CARLIN was born in 1949 in South Africa, grew up in Uganda, went to school in Kenya, and then read English at Bristol University. *Vuyelwa* is a Xhosa name, meaning 'rejoicing at the birth of a girl'. She started writing again about ten years ago, having been a prolific poet as a child. As well as writing, she works as a life model. She is married with two children, one autistic, and lives in Shropshire.

Her poems have appeared in various magazines and have won prizes in several poetry competitions. In 1988 she won 3rd prize in the Cardiff International Competition. A selection of her work is included in *Seren Poets: Two* (Seren Books, 1990) ●

Acknowledgements: *Poetry Durham* and *Poetry Wales*.

The Dragon

He lives in my garden –
Always has, the green
Little dragon – in the corner
Where the old ivied blocks are,
The grass cuttings, –

A quick emerald;
He seldom throat-
Rips with cold fire;
He is quiet and conforming
– Most do not know he is there.

From his rich writhy
Hummocks he drapes,
Though, silkenly,
All my house; his green strange
Thoughts flood mine and me.

Strange Dolls

It used to be commonly done
To make portraits
Of dead children –

Catch the soul –
Fled flesh while still whole:
They hold roses, petals

Pattering the white frocks;
Eyes painted wide,
About the neck

Silver or gold.
– I saw a burial,
Mine, – I was a young child:

Clump-thump
On a white delicacy;
– But I was at home,

Staring from the dresser
– Great sapphire
Eyes owly.

The Drowned Girl

Solid she was, a strapping girl,
but quite dead – white
as purest Carrara, a fine heavy
church Mary: gleaming

as Agamemnon stepped from his bath,
net-caught, his tired mouth
chocked with fruit. A long hairslime
danked down, princess-gold

once, we said, knowingly: now
winter-leaf-black.
Behind great pale basins stoned once-
dumpling eyes, blue-fat.

Monsters

He was beautiful, the monster,
All-powered:
– It was so exciting, making him.

The idea caught on,
And Sunday garages
All rang to the fashioning

Of monsters: each strove
To outblaze
His neighbour's monster eyes,

Outlume
Next-door's clear
Ivory monster skin.

Now they all rumble, soft,
Down-cellared
Among our apples and beer,

Chained with great chains.
– We feed them still,
Despite our fear

Being proud; – and walk them,
Times-ten friends
Must hold the chain,

Terrored: yet we half long
To loose them on the field; – know,
Understand, eat desolation.

Spring Fever

Logitek 100
Asked one day
– How many strawberries
Grow in the sea?

They coded in
As they thought good
– As many as red herrings
Grow in the wood.

Logitek riffles through the files
Lead-slow,
Apple-green characters
Grown pale as straw:

– Must be the Spring
In its chips they plained
– See how the mad buds
Buffet the pane!

It needs a spell in the March
Wind-swirl
Being slapped about
By daffodils.

The Trees

Your grandfather lived in those
Old skywater days;
He had trees in his laden
Garden – limes, alders.

He could go walking
Each tender morning in cool,
Under crowds far
As he could see of leaf-jostle.

He liked to paint them,
– Great giants, you can't imagine
From the films, he said:
Would touch no smidgeon

Of bark-rough or tendril –
He had a fear
They would shrink, green talls,
Ever after from him, destroyer.

They were his love,
The dripping silks bird-called:
– He was a jeweller,
Lately worked in emerald.

Scots Pines

Like inept soldiers,
rank on rank,
tall tatty men,

they seem to march
downhill, backward
gently-leaning:

saturnine
among spring newnesses
pale as wax

they are; patient-
shabby beneath great
snow haversacks.

The Exile

Under the low-slung pearl,
It is quiet and cool
In this mossy bath
Of a country,

This house in whose old
Slaved stones
They will wedge a brass
When I die:

The hugenesses
Are behind me now,
For ever: – mammoth ribs
Of snow-iron,

Black leaf-gum
Of rain-burdened autumn,
Twilight halls
Of larch-feather.

– I am not ungrateful:
Certain beauties –
Evening fire
Gold-molting the hummocks –

Make me stare: but I
Am Tom Thumb,
Tom the frail, in the old
King's gnarly hand-cradle.

Janet Fisher

JANET FISHER was born in 1943 in Birming-
ham, and grew up in the countryside of North
Oxfordshire. She studied Law at Bristol Uni-
versity, failed at teaching, and went into pub-
lishing until her elder sons were born. She
moved to Skelmanthorpe near Huddersfield
in 1978, had a third son, and in 1985 became
seriously ill. After several years she 'decided
that life was for living and hang the consequ-
ences', met a lot of local poets and started to
write herself.

She now co-runs The Poetry Business in
Huddersfield (with Peter Sansom), and has
published two pamphlets of poems, *Listening
to Dancing* (Slow Dancer, 1989) and *Raw*
(Wide Skirt Press, 1990) ●

Acknowledgements: *The Wide
Skirt, Listening to Dancing*
(Slow Dancer) and *Raw* (Wide
Skirt).

Fifty Years On

it's Quiz Night at the Chamberlain Arms and Frank
has written the questions himself this time.
Jane, Irma and I, drinking ginger wine, drying up
on England captains and the length of snooker tables,

squeeze fragments of gossip into the gaps.
The Vicar has been asked to bless the Scout
Hut as a rates dodge, it's part of the job
like praying for the dead and always smiling,

but Jane comparing the Cubs to Hitler Youth is probably
tactless: Irma's father was in the Luftwaffe,
a P.O.W. who stayed on. Irma hates Poles
and Communists. We're into the second half and Frank

is hotting up the humour. Which United player is
a German newspaper? Zy Tung? Dee Velt? The answer
is Gerry Daley, Jane declares it's racist and Irma
pinks up. Later over coffee she pounces on my

Tradescantia. Do let me have a piece of your
Wandering Jew, she exclaims, waving the scissors.

But the difference

> was, she thought, a good woman
looks after others' interests such as grinding
corn, sewing skirts from old curtains,
hunter gathering, whereas a good

poet doesn't give a bugger, stuffs
herself on chocolate and champagne, sucks
dry the gourd of desire, thus releasing
the good poetry locked within. But being

quite well read as well as good she knew
only too clearly the statistics on obesity,
cirrhosis and hepatitis B and so forewent
these pleasures though not without certain

feelings of regret and moral complacency. But
she had a problem and it was this: the good
man whom she loved, who did not know
she was sacrificing good poetry for good

womanhood, who sat up late each evening
in their clean kitchen wrapped in a warm
scarf, writing his memoirs, unaware
of what he had nearly missed.

By the pump dry-eyed

> across from two men and a boy,
flaunt it, written in their eyes,
the sun, the diet, giving her that lightness,
that looseness of hip enough to feel the bite

of lewd stares, and old enough to appreciate it.
Perhaps they were only dozing by the wrenches,
heavy lids drowsy with heat not lust;
perhaps they were merely licking

the dust from their lips. Giddy with fumes,
a shimmer of petrol blurring her gaze,
she slots the pipe and fishes for credit,
pockets the flimsy to show her husband.

Touching Up

He keeps the photos in his briefcase
to hand round when there's a lull.
Laughter changes hands.

He eyes the sullen throat
of the waitress collecting glasses,
her bottom, her narrow waist.
He mouths off to his friends.

Next day in waspish black and yellow
she carves her number on his shiny wing.

Jocasta

And the first time I saw him
like the world after rain,
the old man dead and the young man standing there,
his hair still damp, shrugging
the wet cloak from his shoulders.

Waking from fever, my throat aching,
my body clear as spring water,
head light with a bright intensity like wire,
like diamond. And his eyes,
blue as the Aegean, as lightning.

He rubbed his hands down his thighs
wiping off dirt and blood.
It had been a long ride.

I ordered water but I was there first,
unloosing his sandals, drying his wounded foot
on my new dress. My heart drowning.

We made him our king,
my king. Can you doubt it?

That was twenty years ago; he is as old
as I was then, our children grown.
But it's over. I'm finished with guilt and grief.
I will not give Heaven that satisfaction.
His reddened eyes have healed, his scars hardened.
Someone else must cry for him. My throat is dry.

Jonathan

French homework due in Tuesday scribbled
in red on the back of the hand not holding
the roller-ball slim-line, black ink, he
confidently analyses *Macbeth* with his
favoured stylistic flourishes and gothic
Js. Bulbous tips of fingers, half moon
nails bitten to the quick, scrape raw
nostrils. Grown six inches in a year,
hair like wire, witty with teachers
when he meets them in the supermarket,
he knows how far he can go, they tell us.

Existentialist

Behind drawn curtains in reflecting shades
he sits and strums:

the smell of spitted pig in café windows;
down by the Seine cheap prints for sale. He found
a Degas once, 500 francs, a dancer bending
in a small dusty square. Geraniums.

The Louvre was disappointing though, the Mona Lisa
tucked up behind crowds, guards, the mirror only
of his own small smile. Moustache and beret
were imaginary.

The city breathed cheap wine, Gitanes, couscous,
hump-backed buses where in felt skirts curling
round their thighs the girls waved, kissed, descended
and descended the steps of Pigalle into the Métro night.

A stinking hole, a straw bed, dawn
from a cold gable across red roofs,
hearing the barrowmen hawk in the gutter
their golden onions.

Journey's End

Getting up at half six
I drove off for Dewsbury in the fog
having had two slices of toast and
difficulty in getting my child to nursery.

Negotiating the middle lane in an
ever increasing sense of insecurity
I was hemmed in by an articulated lorry
carrying car axles from Düsseldorf to Newcastle,

causing me unfortunately to miss my junction
so that, abandoned in a stream of traffic,
I hopefully flashed my lights at the XR3i in front and,
he having returned my signal, drew in at the nearest service station.

Needing a shoulder to cry on I sat with him
on a grassy bank overlooking the Happy Eater and when
he put his hand up my skirt and nibbled my ear
life had never been sweeter.

Having renegotiated the carriageway upon
which as it happened the traffic was now thinning out
I found it by a judicious use of the accelerator
possible to get to work only twenty-seven minutes late.

Christine McNeill

CHRISTINE McNEILL was born in 1953 in Vienna, and moved to London in 1970, where she learned English at night school, and later trained as a tutor of ESL and German. She now lives in Cromer, Norfolk, and teaches in adult education.

Her short stories have appeared in *Critical Quarterly* and been broadcast on Radio 4, the World Service and BBC Radio Merseyside. The poems published here have appeared in the magazines listed in the Acknowledgements; others have appeared in *Poetry Durham, Orbis* and *Jewish Quarterly*, and her translations of Austrian poetry have been published in various magazines. ●

Acknowledgements: *Envoi, Foolscap, Iron, London Magazine, Poetry Wales, The Rialto* and *Writing Women.*

Déjà vu

Budapest is like a stage-set.
Solitary benches at the war-memorial.
Effort laid in aspic of flowers.
We cross and recross streets.
'Don't park your car there,'
an old woman in a fur hat stops us.
'Police will be here, even at night, to fine.'
She shows a photo of her grandson. Jeans & sneakers.
'Escaped across a minefield –
but his right leg never managed the West.'

We cared for linen that night.
Freshly laundered, it broke between us.
In the morning, lying beside me as my success,
you tell of a dream in which your face
was an ice-field.
On it a woman was running.
She ran and ran,
but you turned your head
to the left
and the woman couldn't move on.

Close-Up

The old woman at the pond
follows the sinewy arrows of birds.
In her eyes the water parts.
Rainbow crystals wing into a girl,
turning the buttons of her duffel coat.

Her small years fisted into joy
when a thread of silver,
fleeing a bruise of sky, beak held low,
headed in a breath of compass navigation
into the pool of its own shadow.

The water closed.
She stood, staring.
Until a fast melting sun,
a torn button and an adult's voice
recalled her.

Each evening it preys.
A fallen bird, the size of the dead.

Virus

A strangeness in me
an inner curtain
No outward signs, I walk normally
Beyond my window
rain and birds jazz
in a south-westerly.

This coast I've come to
where meanings hinge on the right
turn of the head
and rugs in vacant rooms
are placed
at a precise angle.

So much
and so little.
The cold in me
that breaks out in heat
at the sight of a blue bowl
half-filled, half empty

A pale hyacinth
its infant bloom
wrapped around worn leaves
This, in the refuge of small hours;
knowing an utmost care:
A cat curling into its own breath.

'My daughter'
By a German Mother

She is a writer. Where it all started?
I have always taken care that she could
spell the longest word in the language
correctly. Following that, I do recall
that she could not hear well as a child.
One had to repeat sentences over and over.
A virus, you understand. Her father,
the doctor, treated it with a syringe.
She may have developed what experts
now term 'that ingenuity'. But don't
miscomprehend me, she has talent –
'a rose by any other name,' she said
when she caught me with another man.
Enfant terrible she became, said new
houses were built but the walls inside
were the same. Named us openly in her
literature, even her father, who, Nazi
sympathiser per se, had suffered a heart
attack under a picture of the Virgin Mary.
From then on she hurried from man to man.
Then went with the radicals on rampage.
Flown the nest to throw filth via a rainbow.
But alas, the years disclaim scientific

experiments, the other day I asked her opinion
on a filial matter. She said I were a glass
through which she walked when she could not sleep.
I could not make head or tail. I keep cats
in my room, at the latest count thirty-two,
all stray and in need of love. As for her,
there was a glassy look in her eyes...
could her vision now be affected?

Geography Lesson

He looked out the window when he asked
the capital of Uruguay,
the largest river in China.

He asked us the main agricultural
product of Albania
and still looked out the window.

An aircraft circled in a precise sky.
'Buenos Aires,' Karl said.
'Wrong,' he replied. 'Montevideo.'

We made another effort: 'Yellow River.'
'Can't wait to get away, can you?'
We smirked – *he* could talk.

In his eyes shifted ochre (for the unadventurous),
turquoise for the girls,
aquamarine for the deep ones.

Legs a single bone
he turned and muttered: 'Theresienstadt,
Auschwitz, Mauthausen.'

Then took the rubber,
erased his drawing of Germany
on the blackboard.

We thought him nuts,
a casualty of years of sameness.
But the names clung.

Vietnam. Israel. Nicaragua.
He is dead now, we think.
And watch through our windows.

View from the Window

Lace curtains at half mast, and the street
forking into Heldenplatz. Great-grandfather,
butcher's overall replaced by a black suit,
had pressed his favourite porcelain figurine –
Der Rosenkavalier – at the glass.
The last Austrian Empress had looked up.

For the rest of his life he recalled her eyes
changing from 'metallic precision'
to 'soulful warmth', and before his death,
when the monarchy had long been abolished,
to 'colourful exultation'. Today is her funeral.
Her coffin has been brought from Switzerland.

The auctioneer and his photographer
are compiling an inventory of my possessions.
The Empress was ninety-six. Observers say
that she insisted on the coronation crown.
A replica of fake gems was made.
'Splicer, masher, draining ladle...'

'Keep playing,' she whispered to her great-grandson.
'I did it to please myself.'
Black cars and hundreds lining the pavement.
'Was she so famous?' My piano pupil asks.
Above, in an anaemic sky, there is wounding
and healing...redemption in forgetting.

The auctioneer taps me on the shoulder.
'Der Rosenkavalier – it is chipped.'
I hold it up. 'Here comes the hearse!'
'Shall we take a picture?'
Nothing can be repeated, ever.
'I'll give it to charity.'

My piano pupil stands very still.
'Was she a good Empress?'
A blackbird descends on the neighbour's ledge.
Its orange feet remind me of a sepia photograph:
Great-grandfather had smiled, away from the camera,
while I penitently faced the lens.

Direct Method

Entrepreneur with a calling, he dials a model agency.
An able hand in French industry has put him
in a house on a hill with wall to wall windows.
There he contemplates the visual before the bell tolls.

She walks across the parquet. Porcelain innocent
and *femme fatale*. Equating art with lust she thinks
of her broad ankles. Her skin has that mortuary appeal
which readily turns him to discipline. For hours

he works, inducing her nakedness into a mirror,
her truth into his second body. Afterwards
in bed, he loves her like a pet he can't own.
She stares into him, smiles at that painting

on the other side of the room – a woman on a hairline
precipice, reclining. Her peculiar dressed look.

Drama

He worked with an actor's mind,
imitating the chicken
and miming the cat crossing the road.
When the cat fell ill,
he asked why I fed it fresh chicken,
and wasn't there a conflict of principles
since the chicken was not any less significant

than the cat? – I said the cat was of superior
intelligence and my companion.
He made an avant-garde issue, saying
he wanted to go to Israel and bury the dead.
I told him he was an actor.

We drifted apart after the first night of *Hamlet*.
He played it with studious finesse.
Reviewers raved: 'A Prince of Denmark who turns
his cross into a burning bush.'
A year later he shot his brains out.
My cat was well, but despite several attempts
could not be weaned off chicken.
One night, feeding it chicken liver,
I dropped a piece on my red carpet.
There was a stain of blood.
It was he who'd said: 'Art is not the way,
only the shadow of one's efforts.'

Viennese Remembrance

How silent it is, grandmother remarks
and keeps on talking. The candles on the tree
flicker particles of wonder. 'Blow them out,'
she instructs. We've only lit them because unlit
trees on graves get stolen.

Mutual appendage, we clasp our hands in prayer.
Aware of roots deep below the marble ground
my fingers cramp on this bit of Heimat.
Grandmother judges the Persian lamb coat
on the woman at the next grave to be second-hand.

At home her daughter talks to herself for hours.
Hands have woven my mother's fate.
She hasn't found herself, I say.
She's been inside, whisper the neighbours.
The woman at the next grave genuflects.

I think of coal in a hot stove,
of Black Madonnas who show more than mercy.
We come in the door. My mother plays
'Liebestraum' on the piano.
At the sight of us her hand slips.

A Mystery

I see a mystery on my hands, the young man said:
The domestic cat catches a mouse and injures it;
Studies it at paw's length, hurls it up in the air,
Retrieves it; lets it run, then claws it back;
The play is finished when the mouse is dead,
The cat leaves it; but should the cat turn
And find the mouse gone, it will frantically try
To repossess it; its senses on full alert,
It will not rest until the mouse is tracked down.

A mystery? The young girl asked.
A mystery, the young man confirmed,
Pointing high at the clouds.

A mystery? She turned to him.
Like a gaping hole, he said; to cover it
Is to deny its existence; to plunge down
Could mean never re-surfacing.
You mean something like nature?
She drew a circle in the sand.
Yes, he said, like the sea-bed;
What lies there, what grows?
You mean, that is *us*? She broke off a flower in passing.
Yes, he said, like God, the ultimate mystery;
To imagine anything about Him is self-defeating.

I don't know what will happen, she said.
I don't know either, he said and took her hand;
It's a mystery: the moment I kissed you.

Angela Greene

ANGELA GREENE was born in Dublin, and now lives in Drogheda with her husband and four children. She began to write poetry in 1983 when her family became more independent, and has since had poems published in many magazines. She was a 3rd prize winner in the Bloodaxe Books national poetry competition in 1987, won the Patrick Kavanagh Award in 1988 and was shortlisted for the Hennessy/ *Sunday Tribune* Literary Award in 1989. A selection of her poems appears in the anthology *Trio Poetry 6* (Blackstaff Press, 1990).

The Douglas Hyde mentioned in her poem 'Encounter' was the first president of Ireland ●

Acknowledgements: 'New Irish Writing' in *The Irish Press*, and *Poets Aloud Abu* (1988).

Encounter

In a garden planted
round a lake, she knew
a secret tree, would go there
often; a high hostess to
crows, and ferns knitted over
harled and varicosed roots.

Above a bank, thronged
with tiny things, swung
one low branch to idle on.
There she lay, one neutral
Sunday, satisfied, in a
new daisy-patterned frock;

ears alive to black
mammies scolding overhead,
the moored protest of
the old boat on the lake;
she craved attention. When
progress of people, trespassing

by her tree, fuelled
her childishness, she
jumped down, called her

name then, twirled and
twirled and twirled so
wild she made daisies

flare, and curtsied before
the wrapped-around rug
of a man seated in a
wheeled chair. With bright
coffee bean eyes he smiled.
I like your frock, and

I like your name, child.
My name is Douglas Hyde.
Go, dance your fairy dance.
Dance child dance.
She held her secret
like a daisy holds light.

Cézanne

Scatters pears and apples
onto the rumpled tablecloth
to tantalise; he leaves
the boy in the red vest
propped on his elbow to ponder
that right arm's long reach.
He has in mind landscapes
where trees, rocks and skies
become the spaces
he renders solid with colour.
Massed jewels
would be this vibrant.
He lets his joy flicker
in the pinks, creams and lilacs on a jug,
and tightens the edges of the world
with light. His worst dream
is of a portrait sitter whose features
shift. He struggles with his lust
for a mountain,
purpled and blue-white as a breast,
which he cannot resist.

The Seal Off Clogherhead
(for Min & Ruth, October 1987)

Turns, flips, bobs, is still; teasing
he slides, dives, disappears and
is back riving the surf-board waves.

He is another fantasy
out among the phantom ships.
He tells his secrets to no one.

We drift here, on yellow sand, in heady
autumn heat to watch the Mournes'
blue dip and peak and thrill

to see him again in this same place:
oil-sleek, lamp-eyed acrobat,
thick dark vein to the sea's flow.

Recipe

> *The following recipe was copied word for word*
> *out of an old manuscript recipe book. The exact*
> *date is not known, but one item in the book is dated*
> *1790.*   THE DUMFRIESSHIRE COOKERY BOOK (1935)

DROP BISCUITS: *The far, far famed Lincolnshire Drop.*

7 eggs (the middle-sized ones are proper), well beat up,
18 oz. of double refined sugar sifted twice,
15 oz. of flour dried the day before.
The ingredients must be quite cold.

The quicker in making drop biscuits
the better and lighter they will be – drop them
upon dried cap paper (not warm), with a spoon,
just round them as quickly as you can in the middle.

To glaze them have ready a little double
refined sugar to dredge over them through gauze.
Slip them off the paper with a large bread knife
the instant they come from the oven or the paper
will not come off at all if this is not attended to.

None in England to equal these for beauty
and excellence. It is a little fortune
to gain into this grand secret,
and have been at it for many years to obtain it. Only
just gently stir in the flour; bake 8 minutes.

Terrorist's Wife

A phone-call takes him
into the dark for weeks.
In the mornings, his absence
fills me with dread. I thin my eyes
to watch for cars that come to wait
down in the street. All day
I move from room to room. I polish
each spotless place
to a chill shining. Fear tracks me
like hunger. In the silence,
the walls grow wafer-thin.
The neighbours wear masks –
tight lips, veiled looks, such
fine tissues of knowing.
My mother doesn't visit. I drag
my shopping from the next town.

Once, putting his clean shirts away,
my dry hands touched a shape
that lay cold and hard. I wept then,
and walked for hours in the park.
I listened for his name in the news.
When I looked at our sleeping son
my sadness thickened.

His comings are like his goings –
a swift movement in the night.
At times, he can sit here for days
meticulously groomed; primed,
watching soccer games on TV,
our child playful on his lap.
But scratch the smooth surface
of his mood, and how
the breached defences spit their fire.

Now, when he holds me to him,
I know I taste murder
on his mouth. And in the darkness,
when he turns from me, I watch him
light a cigarette. In his palm
the lighter clicks and flames.
Balanced, incendiary.

Sand

The dunes lean back on the permanence
of bent trees, quarry humps, spires,
sea litter hoisting marram skirts:
gulls flock to feed on the hinged
wastage of land and sea, their cries
hang in still blue air.

Trapped in light, the distant cliff-face
goes on staring:
from the horizon's exact rim
returns the sea
– forever in moon-reined motion.

I wonder at their memory.
They seem so sure of where they are.
What they can do.
I walk the tide's pale lip
into the weathered jaw of years
till even my footprints fade

Liz Cashdan

LIZ CASHDAN was born in London, and now lives in Sheffield. She is a teacher and writer, edits the newsletter for the Northern Association of Writers in Education, and runs workshops in museums and places of historical interest. She is now working on a long poem about Fletcher Christian, for which she has been awarded an East Midlands Arts bursary. She is also finishing a novel based on family history about a woman medical student in Russia before the First World War, a chapter from which has appeared in *Critical Quarterly*. She likes to think of her writing as 'saving bits of the past and present that would otherwise be lost'. ●

Acknowledgements: Staple and Nutshell.

The Loggia

September 1939, summer holiday over
we arrive at the new house.
'There's a loggia at the back,' my father says.
We've not had one before.
I imagine him squatting in the yard
begging for scraps at the door
peering through the window with watery eyes.
Perhaps he'll come round the front
help us with our luggage
down the long lavender path.
But no one lets us in.
My hand grips the stair-rail while
a voice from the wireless declares war.
All afternoon we unpack belongings
round the house; emergency rations
in the garden shelter. That's where he'll sleep
I think and shudder when my father
clicks the lock.
After tea my sisters pin blankets
over windows to protect the dark.
I wonder if he has a gas-mask.
Please God, if there's an air-raid
make them let the lodger in.

After School

Slowly up the cemetery steps
past white marble and sad mottoes
we climb reluctant home.
A hot day, limp cotton dresses
stuck to sweating bodies. Huge girls
in uniform, absurdly bulging.
Ginnie's secrets fall from her fat lips.
'Laureen,' she says, 'I stroked her hair
in Maths today.' We stare.
Horror widens our eyes.
Muscles tighten in secret places
and still we cannot speak.
Our own silence and the hot afternoon
oppress us. We long to touch
and know we are forbidden.
'Her hand on my arm,' says Ginnie,
'I could smell her body.'
Ginnie's hand, puffy pink fingers
still swollen from winter chilblains
moving through Laureen's corn-ripe hair.
We stand and stand but Ginnie says no more.
She yawns, elbows us to break the spell.
'Come on,' she says, 'I want my tea.
It's strawberries today.'

To My Elder Brother

You threw me over your shoulder.
I hated it, hated the upside-down feeling,
Out of control, in your power.
You laughed and your bald head shone.
Once absent-minded, you drank the tea slops
Mother had poured into your cup.
But you didn't notice, you were locked
Into Ximenes, Turkish grammar, Urdu poetry.
For years you worked for Father

Selling wool but hating it.
Every night when I went to sleep
You played Chopin, Brahms,
Mozart piano duets all on your own.
You called me little Schwester,
I stuck my long chin out awkwardly towards yours.
I cut my holiday short for your wedding
Then watched your wife and Mother
Squabbling for love and money.
You had been an old-maid man so many years
We laughed when you called your son
Across the garden, 'Mat, come to Uncle!'
Then deafness and a slouching gait
Led into old age.
'Gout!' the doctor diagnosed your swollen toes.
'Off with his leg,' the surgeon said
But the gangrene had crept too far.
So Jack, you were dead.
In the crematorium your little Schwester
Saw your coffin slide smoothly
Into its secret place.

Cutting Loose

Cut-outs today, her mother said,
Showing her how to manoeuvre finger and thumb.
She remembers those nursery days
Blunt-ended scissors refusing to turn
Neat corners, leaving white half moons
Like unexpected halos.
Sometimes the wilful blades would chop off limbs,
Slit faces in their clumsy surgery.

Now as she sorts and cuts the photographs
Her bungling anger leaves his severed arm
Still guiding hers towards their wedding cake.
And when she has to face the family groups
He's so hemmed in, the others suffer
Lacerations she only meant for him.

Mixed Singles
(from Dürer's engraving of Adam and Eve)

Eve has been wrong-footed
Confined in her less-than-half the picture,
Crook'd arm mirroring the serpent's
Body slither, an apple held
In the fingers of her snake-head hand.
Adam is all male muscle,
His open palm innocent, expectant.
Eve has another apple for him
In her left hand, arm curled
Sinistrously behind her back.

We know who will win:
However Eve serves
The linesman calls fault.

Deconstructions

My hammer will topple a small statue
Nimrod, Nero, Stalin
the name is irrelevant.
A little chisel for chipping at walls
China, Jericho, Berlin
it doesn't matter where
stones come tumbling
down in a dry dribble
of sound.
I will no longer
use my bellows
to puff up the complacent bellies
of little men
who think they're god.

But through the gaps in the wall
come other little men
with swollen heads.

Mary O'Donnell

DEREK SPEIRS

Acknowledgements: *Honest Ulsterman*, *Krino*, *New Irish Writing*, *Oxford Poetry*, *Poets Aloud*, *The Salmon*, *Wildish Things*, and RTE Radio.

MARY O'DONNELL was born in 1954 in Monaghan, Ireland, and studied German and Philosophy at Maynooth College. She has worked as a translator and a teacher of German and English, and is currently drama critic for the *Sunday Tribune* and a freelance broadcaster for RTE. She lives in Maynooth, Co. Kildare.

Her poems have been widely published, and she has won several competitions and awards, including the Writers Award Scheme, Allingham Award and Listowel Writers' Week; she was a runner-up for the Patrick Kavanagh Award in 1986, and a 3rd prize winner in the Bloodaxe Books national poetry competition in 1987. Her first book of poems, *Reading the Sunflowers in September*, is due from Salmon Publishing in 1990, and her short story collection, *Strong Pagans*, from Poolbeg Press in 1991. ●

Uncharted

Once, we dreamed
                    of sailing the Amazon,
alligator-green, watery light, snakes,
with David Attenborough – far, far,
                    from the crannóg lakes
of Monaghan, and we considered the merits
                    of marrying
the German chef d'équipe.
Now we meet perhaps in summer –
                    children, work,
the foibles of husbands, jam-packed
in the bolting phrases of a day or two,
                    and we know how erosion
has deepened those rivers we never travelled
                    with men we have not loved.
Despite time and distance, corners knocked,
part of us is girlish, still rafted
                    in a state of half-want,
well-primed for awkward water,
just in case…just in case…

Border Town

That town seemed comfortless once,
locked in a slither of damp roofs,

wrapped in a winding-sheet of rain,
huckster shops or tattered cabbages,

limp street corners, or
the whine of mechanical saws.

Mothers the shape of soft pillows,
slowly pushed prams, their baskets bulky.

The air was brusque
with the bite of local voices.

Now, when winter scours this plain
like a giant wire brush,

and the wind's a bitch
untempered by rumpled hills,

when people drawl
in morphine-heavy tones,

I look north
to the half-vexed border people,

tongues quick yet awkward,
mood and humour garnered

like nettles beneath the skin.
On a summer market morning

I thought I had ignored, the hills
are goosebumps on nervous terrain,

golden with buttercups,
and the hiccuping streets,

all rise and slump,
are drenched in light.

Histories

1

You can drift through Europe for weeks,
till your eyes glaze from the ache
of stuccoed ceilings, frescoed facades,
poems and dedications in an arc of colour
above a doorway, bannered from one century
to another, like letters of praise.

The perfect clocks in German cathedrals,
all yellow sun and moon, burnished planets,
computed in a space the size of a tablecloth,
a people's soul ticking coherently
in patient mechanics, in slate and stone,
like a message to the future.

Half-dazed by the casual abundance
of cornices, architraves, rose-windows,
you read a story in stone, feel the breath
of incubi from 14th century gargoyles
that dance in a sunlit cupola, perch
on the symmetries of a Gothic arch.

2

Coming home to Ireland is to feel deprived
in the pretty reds of a Georgian square,
the tamed aesthetic of wrought-iron balconies,
to sense this place an afterthought
of recent history, straggled haphazardly
across the ramparts of a few square miles.

It is to drive through a country village,
know every house was once a servant's hovel,
to let your anger leak on rain-sodden thatches,
on scutched acres at the edge of a bog –
written about, loved in lieu of a mistress,
but – for all the cant – triflingly.

3

Ireland reads no glorious hieroglyph beyond
a code of cashels and scarred fields,
mumbling efforts to minister a hunger,
hears no clarions where steep roofs
brush the clouds, or great prisons
are stormed in the name of freedom.

No sense of early birth, or the way
a street is loved for its yellow decay,
the secrets of memory laid down
in generations of tramping feet, or
the bell-flung echoes of those who rushed
to write themselves on history's scroll.

Deprived of a morning chance to admire,
in rites of praise, this place
never stretched its limbs while young,
or sang deep-roofed cacophonies,
loosed reasons to deck itself in pride,
whet its tongue unflinchingly in stone.

Cuckold

One of my legs will not obey,
rejects command as if the muscles
had established independence.
At night I drag it screaming to the window,
watch stars out on a limb
in spidery constellations,
while my wife snores in bed,
sated from her lover,
having coiled with him on the garage floor.
Across my mind a black scroll spreads,
starpicked with nerve-ends of sanity.
The Great Bear paws my crippled limb,
sensing honey in human blood,

Signus slowly pilots
up the stillness of my veins,
dip-headed to untangle fragments
that obstruct the body politic.

Frosted nights are best.
The rebel leg terrorises,
and stars sing their white reply.
By the time my wife moans
what the hell I'm doing,
that inert part has pulsed and warmed,
half-roused as the Great Bear
thunders through the undergrowth,
Orion's Belt shoots sheer across black space,
and my blood is pounding, pounding,
beyond the edge of night.

Signus: The Swan, a distant solar system.

Mer-men, First-form

Elbow to elbow, they prop one another,
rest on the brink as we read poems,
a furry warmth quiescent, nurturant.

Casually, they touch, little mer-men
whom the world has not tried.
They smile secretively, shyly,

loathe to surface, happy seeming
with hints of half-told tales,
treading pale sand at the ocean-bottom

as sunlight flimmers idly
on the ceiling of their dreams.
Clear-skinned, they drift, conscious

in their way, among pink breathing
corals, striped fish or sea-horses,
waters pitching time to make

each moment last for ever.
They will be pried, when the shell
relinquishes, unfurls young men,

will suspect each other at the surface
when pain of midday beats them;
echoes from playful dreams rise,

chorus, till they shed the song
of oceans, stand to face
the hungry beast of adulthood.

The Welcome House
(for Margaret)

An old house this – wide, yellowed.
The south-facing windows
examine spruced hills intently.
It is a happy house.
Insects throng here.
          Hornets, mosquitoes,
          adventurous spiders,
sense invitation, monstrous solidity,
in lichened chimneys or windows
that rattle in an autumn storm.
          Unwanted insects
          emigrate here
from sharp-eyed homes where loitering
is forbidden, gauzy webs brushed,
and mosquito bites mean quinine;
          where toxic sprays wield
          death on little creepies.

Hornets hatch revenge
in the high cedars near the house,
        pool strategies
in crooked chimney-pots.
They plummet by accident,
buzz their puzzlement against
window-panes, until released to the sun.
The house is friendly,
        wears a *welcome* sign for insects.
They find asylum at night,
scuttle relieved, through cracks,
beneath doors or down the walls.
        Sometimes
they waken us, their hard,
glistening backs, rapid legs
        or fragile wings
        noisy
as they make themselves at home.

Girl Warrior

After ten years, I try the veil,
pad slowly around the mirror,
assemble fragments of a girl warrior,
net and strips of satin
whitening her cheek in shadowlight.

What rushes in are the dreams,
like incessant drums, the day
when white marked the boundary
between life and life.
Lace clusters and taut satin,

stern photographs, women
in military smartness,
that passive elegance, intruded
like a fracture at my core.
Today, the white odour of gauze

no longer signals war,
not a little shell hat
with constellations of pearls,
feats of womanhood,
graces and abundances

I was not ripe to display.
Whoever that girl was,
we are now friends.
I tell her white is white,
that seed-pearls and satin

can never speak who we are,
or what we are to do –
whether the world is cracked bone,
or fireworks in a summer garden.
After ten years, I try the veil,

remove it then with equanimity –
no longer a girl, or wanting to be,
well-clear of frontiers
where bones spiked the flesh,
bound by blood and truce

to a white girl warrior.

Old Gardens Are Not Relevant
(a Hungarian woman remembers the late forties)

She was brought to church in summer,
slept in my arms as July
stifled our breath.
We passed perfumed gardens,
ladies, men who stood quietly.
Maids in starched frills
worked like strange butterflies,
while the fields were waving.

There were storks on the smokestacks,
a good sign, they said.
It was a quick baptism,
beneath a blue and yellow cupola.
But she never knew a day's health,
and people asked what birth-devil
sat on her cradle,
what demon regarded my sleep
in the months before.

When she was six,
I brought her back
on the sourest day of the year,
the cupola above in a sheath of frost.
He poured water again,
wished good health on her head,
called the potentest graces
to enter her.
On the way home we stopped,
took tea and cakes in a yellow café.
Again there were ladies,
maids in starched frills.
Outside, a beggar avoided the sleet.
We watched as we ate.
Since then she's never looked back,
strong and wilful as a mother could wish.

I pity women with sickly children.
The smokestacks were crushed,
old gardens are not relevant.
Today, they'd wait a long time
for a second, saving ritual
beneath the infinite lights
of a blue and yellow cupola.

Katrina Porteous

KATRINA PORTEOUS was born in 1960 in Aberdeen, grew up in Shotley Bridge, Co. Durham, and now lives in Northumberland. After reading History at Cambridge, she went to America as a Harkness Fellow for two years, studying at Berkeley and Harvard.

She has won several poetry prizes in Britain and America, including awards in the Arvon, Lincoln, Bridport and Newcastle *Evening Chronicle* poetry competitions. In 1989 she received an Eric Gregory Award. She was recently commissioned to produce a series of "texts for the landscape" for the 1990 National Garden Festival at Gateshead. ●

Acknowledgements: *The Gregory Poems 1987-1990* (Hutchinson, 1990).

If My Train Will Come

If my train will come,
Quietly, in the night,
With no other sound than the slow
Creak of wheel upon wheel;
If, huge as a house but brighter,
Crouched at the edge of the fields
Like a steaming beast, it is waiting
Down the deserted road;
Though the colliery gate and the church
Where my Mother and Father were wed
Are all grown over at last
And the people I knew there dead now,
If a stranger alights
And, holding my breath, I see
That he has your eyes, your hair,
But does not remember me;
And if there follows a girl
With my face from years ago
And for miles by the side of the tracks
The Durham grasses blow –
O, if my train will come
With its cargo of souls who have passed
Over this world to find me,
Will I go? Will I want to?

Factory Girl

Five nights a week I work as a factory girl.
My job's in Necklaces. Cartons of colourful beads
Run down the line and I thread them. The Sorter leads,
Popping them into their boxes – a difficult task,
For sometimes the green look blue, the blue look black,
And many fit all six boxes equally well;
But the Sorter has to be certain they don't get mixed.
Everything's made to fit. The order's fixed,
See, by the day, and we stick to it, or else
There's plenty others wanting jobs...

                           My shift's eleven
At night till the early morning bell drills seven
Into my dreaming. Then I go home to bed.
I don't know whether it's dark or light out there.
In here it's always the same, summer or winter.
With all of our necklaces made to the book, as we thread
In the given order (green today, then red;
Tomorrow, red then green), to me they appear
So much the same; like the nights, the bus-ride here,
The sequence of stop after stop, long as the Tyne,
Counting the lights in the water, the broken line
Down where the shipyards were that went redundant.

I think of the oddest things to unsettle the pace:
Sometimes of Dad. I try to remember his face
And the stories my Mother told me: ('You should've seen
How he looked in his uniform, Hin, when he went to the War!
I don't think I'd ever loved him so much before.'
'What a knees-up we had when the fighting was over! At last
We were done with the sirens, the blackouts and rations. God willing,
He'd still have his job at Swan Hunters.' But that was gone.
'When he heard, he looked like a factory shutting down,
The lights going out in the workshops, one by one...').

Well, I string this together. I try to make sense of the past.
But pieces are all I have. I can't force them to mean
Anything much. I just see what I want to. It seems
A haphazard collection of memories, turned in the telling
This way or that by a whim, as an order's cast;
O, nothing seems to make logical sense any more.
I go home, and I dream of necklaces snapping, beads spilling
Into their moving millions, over the floor.

Kicking Against the Walls

It's starting to break my sleep.
A rich and alien germ
Riddles my body, deep
Inside, inseparable,
Wanting rid of me, kicking
The walls, striking the land
That holds and feeds it. Tell me –
A woman would understand –
What is the worm that quickens
Out of my mould and climbs
Onward to leave me dying,
A traveller in time?
I sing to it in confinement.
Rage, my baby; grow
Strong with the secret, darling –
The dead won't let you go.

Ducks

In their beady dreams among sleepy green sluices,
Water slopping on walls and prim willows,
After a long day's leisurely wallowing,
Niggling, bickering – could they be envious,

Those sleek Cambridge ducks in their comfortable couples;
Pompous in uniform, aggressively sociable,
Well-stuffed with breadcrusts, insufferably jolly,
Awkward on land, on ice, skittled, ridiculous?

Here on the hush of a tide, the seasons' drifting,
Lone Northumbrian eiders dumbly endure
The creeping to bitterness, death-cold and thaw,
Dipping and riding the heave like rafts.

It's said they're the souls of the drowned, cast back,
Free. Like the hermit saint their shag-wings warmed,
No ice flurry ruffles their sea-bound calm.
They gather in darkness. Under the storm's assault,

Buffeted into knots, they stay; then, leaving
No ties, in spring the drakes straggle off in brave,
Vain male huddles, pied surf on black basalt.
She'll raise her brindled brood in the bent alone,

The brown mother eider, minding a neighbour's clan
In shifts; till, soon, into the steep grey waves
She'll pitch her tiny, trusting, buoyant crop
Of woolly ducklings, wildly rocked to sleep.

Jill Maughan

Acknowledgements: *Ghosts at four o'clock* (Bloodaxe).

JILL MAUGHAN was born in 1958 in Newcastle. She grew up in Chester-le-Street and went to school at Polam Hall in Darlington. After stints in journalism and social work, she took a degree in Communication Studies at Sunderland Polytechnic. She worked as publicity officer for Castle Chare Community Arts Centre in Durham, and then as an outreach worker for young offenders. She is now a freelance writer, and lives in Plawsworth, Co. Durham.

She was joint winner of the Newcastle *Evening Chronicle* Poetry Competition in 1984, and won an Eric Gregory Award in 1987. Her collection *Ghosts at four o'clock* was published by Bloodaxe in 1986 as a pamphlet and in the *Fourpack #1* anthology. Her first children's novel, *The Deceivers*, was published by Collins in 1990. ●

Flames

These flames are made to measure,
they jump like poor circus animals
and flicker there

in imitation of the real and dangerous thing.
It's true there is none of the bother
like before,

no scarring red embers which left
such burn marks
I had to buy a rug

to lay over them. I think
people knew what it hid,
secrets are dangerous tools,

and there isn't the mess there once was,
the aftermath of dust and ashes
that powdered the furniture;

now I just flick a switch and get
a red, artificial glow and flames
adjustable to three settings.

It's much safer than before,
there's none of the roar and spit,
a glass door

separates me from all the old risks,
they swore it really was
the ideal solution.

It is strange then how I miss that inconstant
fire but it was that white heat
that saw me through

and in its flicker were my best dreams,
the ones I was willing to scratch
around in the dirt for.

A small death

The cat which no one's bothered to bury
has rotted unceremoniously
at the side of the field.

Each morning we've passed it's faded
a little, become more pained as if
tired by its struggle to remain.

At first we had curiosity, we noticed its patchy
colourings, the way it could have been
anyone's homely pet.

Even its fall into death didn't look
too startling, more as if it were
nudged rudely or jarred into perpetual sleep.

But lately that's all changed, now its fur
has rotted to transparent thin leather
and its mouth stays frozen in a long

lipless scream, its teeth are broken white bars
where the flies enter and the air that chances
to breathe over it is rapidly hurt.

Now our curiosity has fled. We stare
into the morning sun, walk wide
of the rancid air, we try to leave this small death

well alone, but it follows us along our path
and lingers in the corner of our eyes,
like a small stain on white, it stays.

Remembering

Visiting his grave, leaving the turf
flowers richer or reading his diaries,

picking over the words, running
a lonely hand over the ink,

catching the loved airy response of his ghost
haunting you in a public place, able

to make you smile, sigh: photographs
yellowed at their edges, create that need,

to replay the good years with a scene or two
from that heightened film you both starred in –

or standing statue, still alone, just letting
the seasons blow in like worried social workers.

Long shadows

Our shadows lean across
the late winter afternoon,

while the sour wind wraps about my ankles.
It's our transience that drifts

across these bare fields like a fate sealed,
and it's very easy to imagine us gone,

our features mere dust
that long shadows fall on.

Tracey Herd

TRACEY HERD was born in 1968 in East Kilbride, Scotland. She has since lived mostly in or around Dundee, and is currently studying English & American Studies at Dundee University. Her poems have previously appeared in small magazines, but her selection in this anthology is the first substantial publication of her work. She wrote the poem 'Treading Water' after reading Margaret Atwood's novel *Surfacing*. ●

One of the Gang

This Little Red Riding Hood
never found her grandmother's cottage
but instead, wandered lost
in the immense forest
dark as a wolf's belly:
seeing smoke curl
from a strange chimney, she went
timidly to investigate
and found her grandmother's body
disappearing
into the throat of a furnace.
She screamed
but only flames shot out –
ashes drifted about her
like a magician's black cloak
disintegrating.

A clan of wolves
circled the newly dug grave:
Red Riding Hood
wasn't even allowed to mourn –
The flowers she threw
were guzzled by the wolves:

despairing
she gave up the bread and cheese
from her little basket
and lay wearily beneath a large tree.

Finally,
the elusive sun
slipped into focus:
Red Riding Hood
greeted this new dawn
with one grey paw
flung across a dripping muzzle.

After the Impossible Dream

Rubbing sleep from her eyes, cradling
twigs for the fire, she saw a mouse
scampering across the floor.
It ran straight into the fire
and turned to face her
sitting up on its two hind legs,
big as a mastiff
or some sort of Buddha;
its teeth straight and white
as those of a beauty queen.
When Cinderella blinked
and looked again

the mouse had vanished
and on the mantelpiece
above the fire, she spotted an ornament
she couldn't remember
ever having dusted.
It was her little world
in a glass surround.
'My glass slipper!' she cried
and the flames in the grate leapt up
in a heavenly chorus.

She took the glass lovingly
in scarred hands

and hurled it to the floor:
Cinderella,
leaning over her shattered portrait,
picked up a handful of glass
and nibbled the shards
as if they were cheese
and she, the mouse that had pulled the carriage
before it turned into a monster.
She rubbed the flesh ragged
from her wrists, laughing delightedly:
a young girl
waltzing with her Prince.
Her veins shone, emeralds
awash in a sea of rubies;
her body, no longer battered
but a jewel
and Cinderella, not mad
but dead
having played the glass slipper game

to the very end.

In the Dark Museum

In the museum of translucent
blue skins, the exhibits lie
soaking up darkness, flat
as pricked balloons.

The girl with the bruised
eyes was unzipped
from black plastic and laid
out, so that her parents could
identify what was no longer

anybody's daughter.

Treading Water

You claim to have brought me back
from the bleak island –
a hand extended
from boat to land
over water dazzled by sun
over water so deep
I might have been drowned.

You admire the glittering
surface, shades of postcard summer
and breezes cleaving
the water like swimmers
but I grow tired sometimes
of what we can see.

I'm itchy in my own –
and need to get under
someone else's skin:
the water's beguiling:
there's fish and corpses
and death's only two-dimensional
if it's someone else's.
The water's dissolved all features
as if they were sugar
and there's something sweet
in the glance: your own
special brand of pornography –
staple it into your memory,
something bizarre to tell your grandchildren.

You love the jewel-tinged blur,
you love the cheap perfume
in my hair: you shield my eyes
from the sun, but the water's
too vast
even for your huge hands.
You've the imprint of a leaf
spring green,

or the crackle of paper
and I've burned all the scrapbooks.

In your mind you've been blinded
by love and forgetfulness:
I was born here.

The Open Gate

Barley field
spreading a brittle wing
from the quiet road:

I flattened stalks
and lay back
ignoring spiders

which danced on thin stems;
ugly framework
of summer parasols.

Lying in your hollow,
my eyes took in
crocheted clouds

hanging
from bright blue needles:
something stung or jabbed me.

I sucked in acres
of ploughed air.
The sun sweated

and swelled above us.

Twilight on the River Cam

The postcard's caption says twilight,
'Twilight on the Cam'. I was there
but it was a light I never saw
amidst the clouds of our petty arguments,
your academic games. I see you now
pompous on an elderly punt, quoting
the lines of some poem: 'twilight's pretty mirror',
whilst vigorously thrusting the slippery pole
into the river's tangled bed;
sweating thickly, a stale green smell.

There's willows in the picture,
not weeping but drooping.
In this light, they look like strands
of hair, plastered to your head:
if you hadn't been God, or had let me assume
your mantle for a day, I'd have washed it all clean.
I'd have ducked your wide, shiny forehead
into the stream, forcing it down, breaking
twilight's pretty mirror,
cutting your face on the golden slivers
till the sun sank red beneath the surface.

Grit and Snow

ash-tray of the old year:
forget the banal poem
'lipstick on dog-ends'
just see
the blood where I bit
my lip
through winter
through grit and snow
to the soft
plateau of spring.

Christiania Whitehead

CHRISTIANIA WHITEHEAD was born in 1969 in Newcastle. She attended Newcastle Central High School, and has just graduated in English from Magdalen College, Oxford. She has written poetry since the age of 15, and has won prizes in the junior and adult sections of the Newcastle *Evening Chronicle* Poetry Competition. As a result she has been on two Bloodaxe-sponsored Arvon poetry courses, and her poems have been published in the anthologies *Bossy Parrot* (Bloodaxe Books, 1987) and *The Earthsick Astronaut* (Puffin), and in *Oxford Poetry* and *The Echo Room.* ●

Acknowledgements: *Bossy Parrot* (Bloodaxe), *The Echo Room*, *Evening Chronicle* (Newcastle) and *Oxford Poetry*.

The unicorn is a symbol of virginity

Dun brown tomorrow. The unicorn
looks surprised. It had faintly expected
always to stay white.
'Does that mean my horn will
creep back into my head?' whimpers
the miscreant, and it paws the ground
a little, as if in protest.
Tush, rocking horse! You have nothing
but milk teeth to talk with,
you are only the little creature
the woman chuckles with,
when she is feeling holy.
Perched there amongst
the shamrocks and thorn roses –
you were never meant to last,
but came down through the ages
on a prayer cushion or in locket form,
eluding the bonny cavalry
by dint of a streak up a tree.
Mother of Jesus, where did you start?
Of course the horn must go.

From a Saxon monk to his love...

Jessica, Jessica, how could I ever
have forgotten to see you?
You, with your noonday eyes
and river wolf's mouth.
I am clutched from above by your sea-bleached throat
and miraculous three-seeded beauty.

Jessica, be careful. You are so beautiful
old Satan may want you all for his own.
You might be Persephone: trip one day
and be pulled down a hole, searching primroses.

Just now you came out of the river
where you had been to visit
your brother, the sun.
Your luculent rise
outdid his glare,
so he sent you home
to wring out your clothes
with your breasts peering through them
shiny as pale crab's eyes.

Me. Hiding behind this tree?
Hmm, well I am dark red and bitter,
and my mouth at this present moment
is full of the wood of the yew.

I care nothing; watching you
catching and rolling the sea
on your brow,
like a great plough, striking a track
between heaven and earth.
So you leave your white marks on me,
and the rain must not come
to wash them away.
We will pray to God for the sun.

Lindisfarne

Men may very easily put asunder what was never joined:
our song together – WULF AND EADWACER

The north of the island has polar-bear feet.
The marram grass in the dunes there glitters
like the hair on a polar-bear spirit.
When I walk on the shore with faith in my rucksack,
it is no lunch. For there are
no trees.

I built an eyrie, a cairn of stones on the shore
for the sea to mate. To germinate meaning,
itself, from the fact of my eyes. No, no, the sea
is deft to back out. (The bear in the ice,
the black land behind the dunes.)
The sea reads its own language to itself.
The sea leaves the land like two edges of cloth
ripping.

But the men with flatulence and wander-lust,
those Celtic saints, dropping their knotted handkerchiefs
all over the island, they made the expedition
from land into sea. Cuthbert ran from the land
pursued by women; they were foiled on the beach
and turned away; they were made to hate
the idea they had ever wished children.
The seed of the sea has no need of a period
under my glass.

No need of a time in the laundering womb.

Behind the dunes is a black land
which was once burnt. When the smoke lifted,
the little crosses we used to engrave in the heather
had gone. The soles had gone.
We used to keep feet there, and they
had burnt.

Margaret will be a nun soon. She did not want to
walk very far over the island. If the bears
had smelt of heaven (hyssop and myrrh)
it would have been better – if they had had

sap in their eyes, instead of this awful glint.
No, her garden is elsewhere. She leans back
into herself, as though in a chair and sits.
She has ineffable qualities.
                              I carry no
internal provender; I am shards of
wave skin; bear claw; the deep.

In the booth of the cliff are ten precious things:
nine telephone receivers (shells) and a seaweed line.
We call a bite, the sea makes polite
noises on the other end.

Words,
yes
they are
locks, staves, bristles.

They never come. The good guests never come.
The cups have been swept out to sea, the bread dies –
has a second death. Here is skill, and there
is my leather coat – two things which make
the sky back off. Long before, when monks played
on the orange cliff, sky, sea and land sat
at buns. Morning and evening. The first day.

Homily

I am tissue paper thin,
shining like rain
and angry.
This is the third time
that God has not answered me.
I am fractious.

Behold me in the transept
early in the morning,
as white and ready to be
holy
as bottled milk.

I am touchstone, I am
tinderbox. I will strike
my prayers off flint
to make them fly upwards –
I may have to push with
both hands.
I am holy milk, I am
trying to be good.

But you, robust pink stones –
just like the fathers,
with the dimples pressed into your cheeks
by an awareness of latent salt water.
You tell me nothing.
I have come here looking
for cordial,
and you tell me nothing.

There is nothing. Nothing but
the skeletal sunlight,
tapping its death certificate on
the priory gate.

Brutus' Last Song

Caesar's back, and they've built him a throne to sit on.
Get back to nature, Caesar. We've got you a tree stump;
broad as your kingly bottom. Magisterial.
Older than you'll ever be.
And when you rise from your wooden cradle,
black marks upon your robes'll tell the people where you've been.

Ah, but when you sit now, that's really something.
See that bush, like a marvellous African head-dress
full of yellow whips, their tops dipped with blood;
or jugular red-hot pokers, who decided to take a day off
and wave a finger at your majesty.
Why, your majesty, see how, when you sit there,
they radiate around you.

One could almost believe you were going to die.

Anne Rouse

Acknowledgements: *Encounter, London Review of Books* and *London Magazine*.

ANNE ROUSE was born in 1954 in Washington, DC, and grew up in Virginia. After reading History at Bedford College, University of London, she worked for seven years as a nurse, both general and psychiatric, in the NHS, and is currently an employment worker for Islington MIND. She lives in north London.

Her poems have appeared in many magazines. She was a prizewinner in the 1989 Kent Literature Festival and a guest reader at the 1990 Poetry Festival at St Mary's College, Maryland. For six months in 1990 she travelled through North and Central America, and is writing a novel set largely in Mexico. ●

Virginian Arcady

My muse came up from the creek,
taller than a man
in the speckled shade
where crayfish imitate tiny stones
and the brisk water plays.

Reckon it was my muse,
being so ringlety and fair
with a child's eye.
In her head-dress bitter, living grapes
nest on the wild vine.

We strolled the bog paths
from the lower fields,
apart by armslength.
She talked low, reproachful, pretty:
said I don't love her enough.

Round

Out till 4 o'clock dancing, they're
Back on the ward at half-seven from Sligo,
Vigorously turning the sheets.
I can't get up no

A double amputee fell
Off a wheelchair and began to spin
Until we could raise him.
I can't get up

A cancer case, deep yellow, spoke of
The discos at Bart's where he'd been a porter.
We slow slow-danced, I braced him for x-ray.
no I can't get up

The sun floods the sluice room.
The young tree outside is a christening white.
He's drawn up his swollen legs and stopped breathing.
no I can't get up

Neither Luke nor John nor the patron
Of wanderers nor Mary herself help the sister
To dial. Women shriek down the phone.
no

Déjeuner sur l'herbe

Mackenzie's shirtless,
kneeling on rubbery
grass to cadge some Thunderbird
off Dougie, a novice
in translating the
unenunciated word.

He's presided years
over the crisp wrappers
of a bachelors' picnic
on the flattened park verge,
lacing his liquid
takeaways with rhetoric;

This time passing out
calm and cold, as the hunched
accelerating homebound
crowd ward off a hand-out
of rain, eyes evading
the blessed body on the ground,

And the confrères, pissed-
on though they will be, wait
until a man's comatose,
breathing a bourn of mist,
before they ransack
wallet, carrier bag, clothes.

– Given what a round
costs, merely practical:
wheels within wheels, Dougie burrs,
mills within mills it sounds
the way he says it,
as the three of them disperse.

Sacrificial Wolf

The careful suburban dead turn their backs
on this squat of sodden grass
hedged by the Finchley traffic;
the vicar poised like a prowhead
over the shameless pit, answered
by a hectoring gull. It brings back
the afternoons in the dry houses,
the hostels and clinic waiting-rooms,
when you with a cor anglais of a shout

parted the smokers' fug,
flattering social workers with quotes
from Blake, or Wilde, or Krishnamurti –
such was the splendour and disgrace
that only a few of us have come to light
our makeshift Roman candles, bitten shy:
an elegy, my friend, dear wolf,
being just your sort of con.

Row

This is not the language of reconciliation.
A dénouement eludes the words, our grizzled insurgents.
My army mires in an old logging road and has to be rescued.
Your boys whoop down to find the cavalry are ants.

And yet we value peace, its rocking chairs, twin oval
Portraits, the framed aspidistra. Even love wants parameters:
The means to snub bullies, and to live upright.
Our fears ricochet between us. It begins in tears.

Daytrip

We'd left the cameras in the Hertz
But made St P's for the tourist Passion.
I knew one of the trio: permapressed, a little weary –
This is what he did on his vacations.
A few bearded heads bled from the corbels.
We walked by the pleated steps of a temple
In whose maw someone was being tried with flame.

We took in the long galleria before lunch.
Sloan made some remark about art being *vox populi*.
I sent him back to the Excelsior with a flea in his ear.

The roofs stretched out, pale in the heat and peaceable.
Your shoulder touched mine. I could tell you were moved.
The wine and the drowse of pigeons dismissed
Any rancour between us. Rested we'd be as good as gold.

England Nil

The advance to Hamburg broke with all the plans.
Doug spelled them out in Luton Friday night.
Someone had ballsed it up. A dozen vans
Waited in convoy, ringside. Blue and white
We stumbled through. The beer
When we found it in that pisshole of Jerries
Was all we needed. Who won the war,
Anyway? Who nuked Dresden? Two fairies
Skittered behind the bar, talking Kraut
Or maybe Arabic. We clocked the poison
Smiles and chanted till the SS threw us out.
Stuttgart was a tea party to this. One
By one they've nicked us, berserk with fear.
You've been Englished and you won't forget it, never.

Her Retirement

Just a little party, nothing swank,
I told the founder, but you know Mr B.
There are so many of you here to thank.

I leave you the later tube trains, dank
At the hand-rails from a human sea
Dreaming down to Morden via Bank.

I've homed quietly to port while others sank,
By keeping at my stenography.
There are so many of you here to thank.

I scan the backs of houses, rank on rank:
The comfy lamps, the oblique misery
Streaming down to Morden via Bank.

Our gardens keep us from the abyss, I think.
With the cheque I'll buy a trellis, or a tree.
There are so many of you here to thank.

And unaccustomed as I am to drink,
I toast you all who follow me
– There are so many of you here to thank –
In dreaming down to Morden, via Bank.

Springfield, Virginia

Colonels live there, commuters to the Pentagon
In sweetly-named estates: King's Park, Orange Wood.
Springfield proper is a set of asphalt lots,
A catch-all town for realtors and mail.

At Peoples Drug, and the fast-food joints
The hands popping open the cylinders of change
Hail from Vietnam or Nicaragua, arrivistes
Wondering at the sourness of God's people.

The high school kids who used to do the jobs
Were white, immune to history:
Andy Sulick, sheepish in a Big Ranch Stetson hat,
A row of enforced dim smiles at Burger Chef.

Eight hundred graduated in '71. That night
Crawling the back-roads, jumping in and out of
Unfamiliar cars, I found a party at a shack.
A boy mashed me against the lean-to floor.

Along the wooded road lightning bugs flared
Like drunks with matches, seeing their way home,
And whipperwills nagged the sleeper
Until a dawn as pink and blue as litmus paper.

Cynthia Fuller

CYNTHIA FULLER was born in 1948 in Kent. She has lived in Durham for the last ten years, where she divides her time between writing and different kinds of teaching, working on a freelance basis in adult education. As well as teaching literature and women's studies for the Open University, she leads writing workshops and women's courses for the WEA, gives readings and runs workshops in schools and colleges. She has two teenage sons.

She is a member of the editorial collective of *Writing Women*, and her poems have appeared in various magazines and anthologies. She recently received a writer's bursary from Northern Arts to help her complete a first novel. ●

Encounter

The steady drift of rain curtaining her
with the ducks, the dripping trees,
the river moving brown and full,
banks straggling with wet pinks,
the path slipping thick underfoot,
the rhythm of her walking mixing
in the pattering, small animal scuffling.

She saw rain peppering small circles
drawing fish to rise in larger rings,
a duck rolling wet beads over smooth back,
shovel-beak delicately preening
among overlapping browns and creams.

She felt the curl of wet ferns,
the clean mouths of balsam flowers,
beech trunks like stone,
water soaking into black earth
and the roots' deep tangle.

Ahead a blackbird's insistent cry –
she looked beyond the curtaining rain –

a figure running, arms spread for balance,
feet sliding, bruising into undergrowth,
running towards, and the bank shrinking,
flowers fading, and the river moving brown and full,
all rhythm lost in her heart's catch.

She saw the possibility of ending here –
rabbit-punched, knifed,
hands on her throat cutting off life –
button-eyed ducks would turn their heads
at her screams, would edge their brood
into the water, orange feet paddling.
She saw her body floating broken,
dragging at the reeds.
Flickering fish would mouth at her,
bob and nudge at swollen skin,
all that was left would sink then,
heavy and discoloured among the stones.

She watched him nearing,
breath tearing ragged, feet heavy,
dark hair slicked smooth, broad shoulders,
coat open, mouth loose for breathing,
young man running.
She did not see him – whose brother,
cousin, father, what woman's son –
only fear, bones near the surface,
blood beating, the possibility of ending here.

And he passing taking
the naked shock of it –
later he thought of the wild eyes
of a rabbit trapped in headlights.
Stumbling, off-balance,
not looking back, but remembering,
later it haunted him what she saw.

She listening to her heart
watched the moment pass with him.
No part of river now or morning,
all links lost she knew herself
caught in herself, alone.

Cassandra

When he understood the power
he'd given her he spat
into her mouth, venom
seared, melted – not her vision,
her credibility.

She wandered the battlements,
her mind flickering
with wars and death.
The future smouldered in her words.
No one believed her.

This Cassandra's seventeen,
school-uniformed and urgent.
Her eyes are fire –
the Trojan battlements
a public speaking contest.

The words she speaks
conjure disaster,
a world that burns,
the gas shield torn,
her universe at risk.

She wins the prize –
for poise, delivery – not truth;
her words defused,
fierce prophecy diluted
in polite applause.

Pool

I have been this way before,
the path jarring across hot rocks,
edges falling in a dusty scramble,
high cracks hung dry with rasps of plant;

the light too bright,
memory of yesterday's waves
engraved in hard sand lines.
I knew the midday tricks of sunlight,
sparkling a glint of water out of air.
I have been this way before.
Today the hard rocks opened on a pool
salt green and deep as any fantasy.
The water fits close.
The weed fronds cling
feathering against bare skin.
The light floats silver wet
as the opal silk of oyster shells.
This is the touch my skin was aching for,
this is the place I never dared to dream.

Beginning

Being roused, uncurled,
squeezed tight along the tunnel,
pushed out from warm blood walls
from darkness into glare,
cold open space;
bones giving, lungs thinning,
sounds beating, touch bruising,
throat and mouth opening
to the taste of our own cry –
we do not remember this.

Waking suddenly, being snapped
from sleep to consciousness
I have felt grief tight in my chest,
a cold grey weight I want to howl
out of its deep lodging, an old pain.
Beginning came before we had
the words to tame it with.
Hurtled again across that line
from not-knowing to knowing
I understand that it is safer to forget.

Crossing the Edge

Mid December and the season comes clean.
Last night the cut-out clarity of stars
declared it, today the world snapped brittle white.
There is an urgency about the birds,
a flurry of shallow flight, a foraging.
Autumn confused us, mushing the passage;
my breath's cold haze tells me where I am.
We have crossed the edge – no more excuse
for the bulbs or me to send brave shoots
unseasonal, into freezing air.

Self-centre

Today I failed to see you
when the sun shone naked
from the bluest sky,
the water clear enough
to show the rocks.

The equivalent centre of self
George Eliot called it,
reserved her sharpest words
for those who missed it,
who only saw their own small selves.

In my scale too it weighs
like lead, this blindness,
a muddy kind of failure,
like crushing the fine blue
of a bird's egg underfoot.

Lavinia Greenlaw

LAVINIA GREENLAW was born in 1962. She grew up in Essex, and in London where she still lives. After studying English at Kingston Polytechnic – when she was also a singer in a band – she took a postgraduate diploma at the London College of Printing, and then worked in publishing as an editor for several years. She has recently joined the Literature Section of the South Bank Centre.

Her poems have appeared in various magazines, and she won an Eric Gregory Award in 1990. She is currently co-editing an anthology of poetry about the environment for Virago and finishing her first collection. ●

Acknowledgements: *The Gregory Poems 1987-1990* (Hutchinson, 1990), *Iron, Stand* and *The Wide Skirt*.

The Death of a Butcher

Did he tell jokes?
Only the ones that were allowed.
(Interview with the widow of a butcher killed
during the Romanian Revolution, 1989)

He delivered meat to the secret police, slabs
of rump and silverside, plump velvety offal.
He knew the taste only by the blade of his knife
but carried the smell home on his fingers
to his wife who cooked soup and dreamed
of infidelity. Good days had some flavour:
heart, belly, brains or tongue.

There'd been some talk, a little broken glass,
then they came for the priest. The village erupted.
He said nothing of a god as he pulled on his boots,
he had no answer for her question
but wandered to the square to join a crowd
drawn by each other's determination.

His name is always mentioned now
when anyone speaks of the first bullet
and those who were not there come to her
for a souvenir of his motivation.
She opens the door and offers what she can:
heart, belly, brains or tongue.

The Innocence of Radium

With a mind full of Swiss clockmakers,
she took a job in a New Jersey factory
painting luminous numbers, copying the style
believed to be found in the candlelit backrooms
of some snowbound alpine village.

Holding each clockface to the light,
she would catch a glimpse of the chemist
as he measured and checked. He was old enough,
had a kind face and a foreign name
she never dared to pronounce: Sochocky.

For a joke she painted her teeth and nails,
jumped out on the other girls walking home.
In bed that night she laughed out loud
and stroked herself with ten green fingertips.
Unable to sleep, the chemist traced each number

on the face he had stolen from the factory floor.
He liked the curve of her eights;
the way she raised the wet brush to her lips
and, with a delicate purse of her mouth,
smoothed the bristle to a perfect tip.

Over the years he watched her grow dull.
The doctors gave up, removed half her jaw,
and blamed syphilis when her thigh-bone snapped
as she struggled up a flight of steps.
Driven by her infidelity, the chemist pronounced

the innocence of radium, a kind of radiance
that could not be held by the body of a woman,
only caught between her teeth. He was proud
of his paint and made public speeches
on how it could be used by artists to convey

the quality of moonlight. The chemist displayed
these shining landscapes on his walls,
kept his faith but lost his life alone in a room
full of warm skies that broke up the dark
and drained his blood of its colour.

His dangerous bones could not keep their secret.
Laid out for x-ray, before a single button was pressed,
they exposed the plate and pictured themselves
as a ghost not a skeleton, a photograph
he was unable to stop being developed and fixed.

Hurting Small Animals

It was the worst party I'd ever been to.
People sat round listening to Elton John
on the radio and talking about pot plants.
She was familiar, used to go out with a friend,
so I thought we'd leave and go for a drink.
It was election night, the first time she'd been
old enough to vote. Her choice was 'tactical'.

God only knows what got her started
about her brother and how she'd once let him
ride a bike over her tortoise and shoot it
with an air rifle; how he'd dared her
to cram bare feet into boots full of frog spawn.
In summer, they stoned crabs on the beach
and glued flies to window-sills. She once

caught a puppy with a skipping-rope handle
and broke its leg, but that was an accident.
The more she talked the more I wanted her mouth
so I bet her I could take her bra off without
unbuttoning her dress. Before she'd stopped laughing
I held it in my hands and this man came over,
gave her a quid, and said it was a good trick.

We went outside and I fucked her in the car park
but it was no good, she got a bit loud
and I had to tell her to calm down.
We met once again, on my birthday.
I told her not to bother getting me a present
and she thought this was the funniest thing
she'd ever heard. After that I was busy.

He wanted someone to cook chicken

and lick the grease from his fingers
but she walked out alone in the forest at night
then stood by the bed pulling dead leaves from her hair.
She could see through his half-closed eyes and was glad
that the bracken scratches burned into her legs
giving her something she could really feel.
Once he tried to go after her but could not
keep up and he fell, suddenly aware
that he had let the dark get behind him.
Later, he watched her sleep and was scared
by the unusual strength of her back.

The next morning they sat down to talk
at a table filled out with years of dirt.
He managed a few words then let his fingers
find a knife to run along each ridge and crack.
For an hour she tried to find a way into his silence,
then went to the window and drew mountain after mountain
on the glass. At last he laid the knife down
and crossed the room in two maybe three paces
to gently hold her head in his hands.
He was interested in how the richness of the bruise
made her face look so plain.

Sex, Politics and Religion

Her features unfold as she lowers her head
back against the basin. I play for time,
getting the temperature of the water just right.
I have almost grown used to touching old hair
and have learnt to respect a customer's face,
clamping my free hand against the forehead

and forcing the spray tight against the scalp.
I must keep my eyes on my fingers
and must not stare at her feathery cheeks
or the rolling chin that falls away to reveal
her puckered throat and the seamless hole
through which she now has to breathe.

If I understood the words burped into shape
by her new oesophagal voice, I might
ask about cancer and what would happen
if my hand slipped and the harsh foam
dribbled comfortably down a network of gullies,
or if a fly…I have to get a look.

The opening is neat and dark,
framed by skin of an unbearable softness.
She has shut her eyes and is smiling
as I massage hard and keep my mind
on the three things I was told by my mother
that a hairdresser should never discuss.

The Chapel Snake
(Tenby, West Wales)

People stopped coming here to pray
so the pews made way for aquariums.
Tropical fish embroider the light,
flex their colours, test the effect
on water on glass on old Welsh stone,
each layer of the world a possibility.

Upstairs, tarantulas crouch, playing dead
if a holidaymaker glances in their direction.
A man rests by a stained-glass window.
He smiles first at Mary and Jesus then turns
to include a welcome for the reptiles.

All the funerals I've been to here...
He clutches a handful of souvenir plastic,
a gift for the girl who had never seen a python
until this one, taken from its tank
to slide round her chest. She is unperturbed:
Go on, touch it. It feels just like a handbag!

Anchorage

The fish factory wriggles free of the Baltic
and takes a firm grip on the North Sea.
Echo and sonar are its spider's web, so fine
they can snare a single cod at a thousand feet.

Trawler crews used to taste the air
then lower a lead weight coated with grease
thick enough to bring back the sea bed;
rock, shell or sand was all they wanted.

Grey steel on grey water under grey sky
moving west with the weather map:
Viking, Fair Isle, Hebrides, Malin,
murky republics bound by salt and oil

carry the Russian sailor to meet dry land
where two years and seven hundred miles
have brought me to your wedding.
The streets are too wide, the houses too small

and I'm scared of getting my face wet.
We run into each other's arms,
our hands reveal a brother and sister
of rock, shell, sand. I am close enough

to see the tear form and melt in your eye.
Inch by inch the Russian sailor
studies the horizon. It never falters.
The ground stays still beneath his feet,

he needs a drink. The cargo is packed
in eighty-pound blocks of suspended animation:
huge, beautiful fish taken from the nets
and returned to water but not enough water.

*

I get tired of whale song and head south
away from five-hour nights and a blazing moon
that tricks me into thinking up mysteries.
Close to the Arctic nets cast up
uncertain shapes. The North Pole wavers.

Those seven hundred miles are back in place
but confetti falls from me with every step.
I cannot get it off my hands
this mess of salty, almost silver scales
leeched in a moment of helpless intimacy,

these leftover scraps of faded tissue
once strong enough to carry the ocean.

North

That skin wasn't made for this weather
and cannot be cured. It retains
the softness of a new bruise.

Only your hands reveal the pull
of an eight-mile post-round over the hills,
leaving clues house by house.

Seventy miles to town once a month
for things that don't need a fridge.
In between there is bread and bread.

Sheep sit in the road causing accidents.
One swerves past, tripping over its guts
in the panic to find a way out.

That dog will be shot by a man
who cleans the heel of his boot
on the purple palace of a jellyfish.

The river's lifeline pins a mountain down
and feeds you yellow flowers
that spill from your front door

but what I hold in my heart is your son,
star-blond on the seashore,
his hands full of stone

that could never be a perfect round
but will dress itself in circles
as it breaks the water and breaks the water.

Your landscape reads like a palm that held ice.

Off the Map

The motorway offered
no perceptible curve,
just a straight line
back into marriage.
On the seat behind,
four kids stung by
salt and sand were
dreaming and hurting
each other. The sky
filled the windscreen,

it was how he imagined
the dead weather to come.
It was easier than he thought
to pull over, mutter something
about needing a piss
and walk. No one
can remember the place.
No landscape. Only
the despair of a woman
who knew the right words
but could not say them
without losing herself,
and the children
beginning to understand,
wanting to be back on the map
but nevertheless trying on
the discarded clothes
of strength and silence.
Three days later
he was back in place,
trying once more to live
with his wife's straight back
and the excuse it gave him
to dirty his hands.
The story is he
went to a monastery,
banged on the door
in the middle of the night,
having left no trace
sufficient for police dogs
or a stumbling two-year-old son.
The children never asked
where he had been.
Each of them gave him
those three days of their lives.
They knew that it was
not a lot to give up.
Just three small circles.

The Gift of Life
Dr William Pancoast, Philadelphia, 1884

In March I inseminated the wife
of a Quaker merchant who was childless.
Extensive tests had led me to believe
that the cause of her infertility lay
in the merchant's limited production of sperm.
His wife was brought to the hospital
for a final examination during which
chloroform was applied to the face and mouth.
This led to complete unconsciousness
facilitating the insertion of a speculum
and the dilation of the uterine canal.
My finest student provided the sample,
applied with the aid of a rubber syringe
commonly used for agricultural livestock.
I also took the additional precaution
of plugging the cervix with cotton rag.
It is now the day after Christmas.
I heard this morning the merchant has been
blessed with a son. God's will be done.

BLOODAXE BOOKS

Winner of the Sunday Times Small Publishers' Award 1990

'Bloodaxe Books has established a ferocious reputation as a publisher of ground-breaking modern poetry. It has cornered a market in the publishing industry with flair, imagination and conspicuous success' – SUNDAY TIMES.

Bloodaxe Books is an international literary publishing house based in Newcastle. As well as publishing famous names in literature from all over the world, Bloodaxe has discovered and helped establish the reputations of many of Britain's most promising new writers, and now publishes more new poetry books – and more women poets – than any other British publisher. Its list also includes modern fiction, politics, photography, drama, biography and literary criticism.

SELECTED TITLES

BLOODAXE BOOK OF CONTEMPORARY WOMEN POETS, *edited by Jeni Couzyn*
Large selections – with essays on their work – by leading poets: Fleur Adcock, Jeni Couzyn, Ruth Fainlight, Elaine Feinstein, Elizabeth Jennings, Jenny Joseph, Denise Levertov, Sylvia Plath, Kathleen Raine, Stevie Smith and Anne Stevenson.   240 pages: £7.95 paper.

FLEUR ADCOCK: *Hotspur*
A ballad telling the story of Northumbrian hero Henry Percy – as viewed by his wife Elizabeth Mortimer. Written for music by Gillian Whitehead, with monoprints by Gretchen Albrecht.   28 pages: £2.50 pamphlet.

FLEUR ADCOCK: *The Virgin & the Nightingale*
Medieval Latin poems with Adcock's witty translations, mostly about birds and young women, including the brilliant erotic poetry of Peter of Blois. 'Lively, rude and eminently readable' – ADRIAN HENRI.   96 pages: £5.95 paper.

ANNA AKHMATOVA: *Selected Poems*
'McKane's Akhmatova versions are unparalleled, and a great advance on his admittedly brilliant early work on that wonderful poet...a restrained brilliance and an extraordinary personal power' – PETER LEVI.   336 pages: £7.95 paper.

CONNIE BENSLEY: *Central Reservations: New & Selected Poems*
'Her poems are sharp, intelligent, vulnerably immaculate, and they make much of their impact by pulling the shreds of whatever carpet remains from under your feet' – JOHN MOLE, *Encounter*.   128 pages: £7.95 pages.

ANGELA CARTER: *Come unto these Yellow Sands*
Four radio plays, one to pictures by the mad painter Richard Dadd. Includes *The Company of Wolves, Puss in Boots* and *Vampirella*.   160 pages: £4.95 paper & £12.95 cloth.

EILÉAN NÍ CHUILLEANÁIN: *The Second Voyage*
The Selected Poems of one of Ireland's most popular women poets. 'Her dreamlike world is haunting, alien, full of awe' – EIRE-IRELAND. 64 pages: £4.95 paper.

JENI COUZYN: *Life by Drowning: Selected Poems*
'In this tough-minded, angry, generous, tender book, we see the stretch of a woman's mind over the territory of our collective lives...chastening, exhilarating, and deeply moving' – ROSEMARY SULLIVAN. 208 pages: £7.95 paper.

HELEN DUNMORE: *The Raw Garden*
'A celebration of nature as it is and as it has been made by man...This is a poet whose words can be savoured on the tongue' – IAIN CRICHTON SMITH. Poetry Book Society Choice. 80 pages: £4.95 paper.

HELEN DUNMORE: *The Sea Skater*
'She seems able to poach subliminal forebodings at will, and suddenly we are in that hallucinatory other-world, sharing her viewpoint' – POETRY REVIEW. Alice Hunt Bartlett Award. 64 pages: £4.95 paper.

LAURIS EDMOND: *Seasons & Creatures*
'She deals with topics people care about – love of all kinds, family relationships, loss, ageing, the fragility of happiness' – FLEUR ADCOCK. Commonwealth Poetry Prize. 56 pages: £4.95 paper.

EVA FIGES: *Days*
Major contemporary novel by the author of *Patriarchal Attitudes*. 'It has a kind of violent stillness, great turbulence beneath a surface calm' – GUARDIAN. 128 pages: £3.95 paper.

SYLVA FISCHEROVÁ: *The Tremor of Racehorses*
'Her Czech experiences have made for a poetry whose surface surrealism protects an underlying satirical vision of considerable edge' – JOHN LUCAS, *New Statesman*. Translated by Jarmila & Ian Milner. 80 pages: £5.95 paper.

PAMELA GILLILAN: *That Winter*
When Pamela Gillilan's husband died, she wrote a series of incredibly moving elegies, after writing no poetry for 25 years. Commonwealth Poetry Prize, first collection. 64 pages: £4.95 paper.

DOROTHY HEWETT: *Alice in Wormland: Selected Poems*
'Many women have been forced into silence, or into disguise and evasion, trying to write poems like these...If the sheer range of grief, ecstasy, pain and love seem incredibly dramatic, that is a good thing' – GWEN HARWOOD. Edited by Edna Longley. 96 pages: £6.95 paper.

FRANCES HOROVITZ: *Collected Poems*
'Frances Horovitz inherits the mantle of Kathleen Raine and of Frances Bellerby. It is an honour to be able to say that her voice is not that of the "age" but of the earth' – ANNE STEVENSON. 128 pages: £7.95 paper & £14.95 cloth.

KATHLEEN JAMIE: *The Way We Live*
'Jamie's gusto for life is colossal, but it is the more infectious for being so unconditionally expressed' – TLS. 'One's duty is just to read her poems' – PETER PORTER, *Observer*. Scottish Arts Council Book Award. 56 pages: £4.95.

KATHLEEN JAMIE & ANDREW GREIG: *A Flame in Your Heart*
The story of the all-too-brief love of a Spitfire pilot and his girl, written by two young Scottish poets born after the war. 96 pages: £4.95 paper.

JOOLZ: *Emotional Terrorism*
'The flame-haired bard of Bradford and often brilliant chronicler of life as lived by the less fortunate...School poetry was never like this' – Q.   64 pages: £4.95 paper.

JENNY JOSEPH: *Persephone*
'*Persephone* reminds me of nothing else. It is itself...Joseph takes the myth of Persephone and makes a litany of it' – ROBERT NYE, *The Times*. James Tait Black Memorial Prize.   304 pages: £6.95 cloth.

JENNY JOSEPH: *Selected Poems*
'Dry wit and acute feeling for the comedy of things inform Jenny Joseph's poetry. She is fast becoming one of our leading women poets' – DAVID WRIGHT, *Daily Telegraph*.   160 pages: £7.95 paper & £14.95 cloth.

SYLVIA KANTARIS: *Dirty Washing: New & Selected Poems*
'Not only a sensitive lyricist but also a speaker of painful truths, a satirist, a poet who can fuse the colloquial and the elegiac, the factual and the surreal...a versatile poet of penetrating vision' – JAMES AITCHISON, *Glasgow Herald*. 128 pages: £6.95 paper & £14.95 cloth.

SYLVIA KANTARIS & PHILIP GROSS: *The Air Mines of Mistila*
'A Poetry Book Society Choice, and one can see why. Quirky, riddling and fleet of foot...a very enjoyable volume' – SUNDAY TIMES.   80 pages: £4.95 paper.

JEAN HANFF KORELITZ: *The Properties of Breath*
'A remarkable depth and generosity of feeling, a readiness to listen for what is submerged...a strain of demonic intensity' – AMY CLAMPITT.   56 pages: £4.95 paper.

DENISE LEVERTOV: *Selected Poems*
Large selection by 'America's foremost contemporary woman poet (LIBRARY JOURNAL) covering all Levertov's books except *Oblique Prayers* and *Breathing the Water*.   192 pages: £7.95 paper.

DENISE LEVERTOV: *Breathing the Water*
'Poetry that with personal honesty acknowledges despair and points to the sources of strength and hope...a commitment to "breathing the water", to being human here' – GILLIAN ALLNUTT, *City Limits*.   80 pages: £5.95 paper.

DENISE LEVERTOV: *Oblique Prayers*
'The first great poetry committed to an awareness of the crisis in human rights in our time, "political" poetry, disturbing, intensely moving, and poetically true' – SUNDAY TRIBUNE (DUBLIN).   80 pages: £5.95 paper.

MARION LOMAX: *The Peepshow Girl*
'There are passionate emotions in these poems, sometimes guarded and obliquely expressed, but Marion Lomax has access to a wide range of voices as well as her own' – RUTH FAINLIGHT.   64 pages: £4.95 paper.

JILL MAUGHAN: *Ghosts at four o'clock*
'Characters steal into these poems in disguise – as ghosts, as animals, recalled through old letters – but Jill Maughan's skilful mixture of terse verse and lingering lines makes them doubly memorable' – DIAL-A-POEM.   16 pages: £1.50 pamphlet.

DEBORAH RANDALL: *The Sin Eater*
'Gutsy, fiery and sensual in its dealings with the basics of life and death...Hers is a deft and womanly art, as direct and disorientating as a ride on the Big Dipper' – SYLVIA KANTARIS. Poetry Book Society Recommendation, Scottish Arts Council Book Award.   64 pages: £4.95 paper.

IRINA RATUSHINSKAYA: *No, I'm Not Afraid*
Why was a 28-year-old woman sentenced to seven years' hard labour for writing these poems? Second edition, translated by David McDuff, including documentary material.   144 pages: £5.95 paper & £12.95 cloth.

IRINA RATUSHINSKAYA: *Pencil Letter*
Poems written in the women's labour camp where Irina was imprisoned for four years. Translated by Lyn Coffin, David McDuff, Alan Myers, Carol Rumens, Richard McKane and others.   96 pages: £4.95 paper & £10.95 cloth.

MARIA RAZUMOVSKY: *Marina Tsvetayeva*
The most comprehensive biography of Tsvetayeva available in any language – improved and expanded from its previous German and Russian editions, and illustrated with over 20 photographs. Translated by Aleksey Gibson. 512 pages: £25 cloth.

CAROL RUMENS: *The Greening of the Snow Beach*
Russia under glasnost: a "scrapbook" of poems, drawings, photographs, and a diary of a visit to the Soviet Union. Poetry Book Society Recommendation. 80 pages: £5.95 paper.

JO SHAPCOTT: *Electroplating the Baby*
'She turns the notion of the private life inside out and plays all sorts of tricks with the imagination' – TOM PAULIN. First Prize, National Poetry Competition. Commonwealth Poetry Prize, first collection.   64 pages: £4.95 paper.

EDITH SÖDERGRAN: *Complete Poems*
Finland's greatest modern poet. The driving force of her visionary poetry (written in Swedish) was her struggle against TB, from which she died in 1923, aged 31. Translated by David McDuff.   208 pages: £7.95 paper.

PAULINE STAINER: *The Honeycomb*
'So authentic an imaginative utterance as to have about it the inevitability of true art' – JOHN LUCAS, *New Statesman*. Poetry Book Society Recommendation. 96 pages: £5.95 paper.

MARINA TSVETAYEVA: *Selected Poems*
'One of the great poets of the century. David McDuff's translations are very good. This is all the more remarkable because, like the poems they translate, they rhyme' – GUARDIAN.   160 pages: £7.95 paper.

For a complete catalogue of Bloodaxe titles, please write to:
Bloodaxe Books Ltd, P.O. Box 1SN, Newcastle upon Tyne NE99 1SN.